C-17 ULTIMATE AIRLIFTER

Flying into Aviation History

For 17 days in August 2021, the world's attention was focused on the Afghan capital, Kabul, as the United States and its allies tried to evacuate thousands of desperate civilians from the city as Taliban forces closed in.

Time and again, television footage showed Boeing C-17A Globemaster III, lifting off from Kabul's international airport with their cargo holds jam packed with hundreds of refugees. The desperation of the refugees was brought into stark relief when several tried to climb onboard a taxiing C-17 and then fell to their deaths as the aircraft took off. Out of 120,000 people airlifted out of Kabul, just over 97,000 flew to safety onboard C-17s of seven air forces.

In *C-17 Ultimate Airlifter* we look at back at the origins of the C-17s in the 1970s and then tell the story of its developments over the following decades.

We then describe the aircraft, looking at its unique features and amazing performance that allows it to deliver super-sized cargos on to dirt air strips, as well as drop hundreds of paratroopers into combat zones, at night.

The global operators of the C-17 are also examined, and we look at their most high-profile missions that have changed aviation history.

Your editor first flew in the C-17 back in January 1996 during the aircraft's first operational deployment to war-torn Bosnia. The giant aircraft appeared to land on a stretch of runway that would have challenged far smaller aircraft. Then a huge Bradley combat vehicle emerged of the aircraft's rear cargo cabin and drove off into nearby woods to join the US Army units protecting the airbase.

The crew were rightly proud of their aircraft impressive performance and over the following three decades, the C-17 delivered time and time again in crisis zones around the world.

Over the years, the C-17 picked up a unique nickname from its crews. It is known as the 'Moose'. I once asked a C-17 crewman if this was due to it being big, strong and a heavy load carrier. Far from it, apparently it is due to the sound the aircraft's pressure relief vents make during refuelling, which mimics that of the sound a female moose makes to attract a mate. That is a sign of the real affection that the C-17 is held by its crews.

Tim Ripley
Editor

LEFT: During its careers, C-17s have flown missions in extreme environments, from jungles, deserts, mountains and jungle. Canada's CC-177s regularly fly missions into the Arctic Circle. USAF

LEFT: Tim Ripley and a Qatari C-17 at this year's Royal International Air Tattoo. Drew Toynbee

BELOW: The USAF's uses its C-17 for global power projection, dropping airborne forces to seize strategic objectives. USAF

C-17: THE ULTIMATE AIRLIFTER

Missions – Squadrons – History – Prototypes

The rescue of more than 95,000 civilians from Kabul in August 2021 was the highpoint of the C-17's career. *MoD/Crown Copyright*

The USAF's C-17s routinely cross the Atlantic and Pacific oceans to sustain America's military garrisons overseas. *USAF*

USAF pilots train to fly in massed formations during missions to conduct massed parachute drops by US Army airborne troops. *USAF*

ABOVE: A C-17 of the 445th Airlift Wing is lit up during the Experimental Aircraft Association AirVenture firework display in Oshkosh in Wisconsin in July 2024. USAF

RIGHT: Air-to-air refuelling gives the USAF's C-17 force global reach. USAF

FAR RIGHT: C-17s crews have to work as teams to achieve the USAF's airlift mission around the world. USAF

ISBN: 978 1 83632 151 4
Editor: Tim Ripley
Data and photo research: Joe Ripley
Senior editor, specials: Roger Mortimer
Email: roger.mortimer@keypublishing.com
Senior editor, this edition: Paul Sander
Cover Design: Steve Donovan
Design: Panda Media
Advertising Sales Manager: Sam Clark
Email: sam.clark@keypublishing.com
Tel: 01780 755131
Advertising Production: Becky Antoniades
Email: Rebecca.antoniades@keypublishing.com

SUBSCRIPTION/MAIL ORDER
Key Publishing Ltd, PO Box 300, Stamford,
Lincs, PE9 1NA
Tel: 01780 480404
Subscriptions email: subs@keypublishing.com

Mail Order email: orders@keypublishing.com
Website: www.keypublishing.com/shop

PUBLISHING
Group CEO: Adrian Cox
Publisher: Steve O'Hara

Published by
Key Publishing Ltd, PO Box 100, Stamford, Lincs, PE9 1XQ
Tel: 01780 755131 **Website:** www.keypublishing.com

PRINTING
Precision Colour Printing Ltd, Haldane,
Halesfield 1, Telford, Shropshire. TF7 4QQ

DISTRIBUTION
Seymour Distribution Ltd, 2 Poultry Avenue,
London, EC1A 9PU
Enquiries Line: 02074 294000.

BUILDING THE C-17

Creating the World's Airlifter

ABOVE: Boeing's contender in the Advanced Medium Short Take-off and Landing Transport (AMST) project was the YC-14. USAF

BELOW: The C-17 prototype T-1 takes off from Long Beach for the first time on September 15, 1991. Boeing

Today, the Boeing C-17A Globemaster III is universally admired for its superlative performance and track record of operational success. However, this was not always the case.

Back in the 1980s, when the C-17 was being designed and built by the then McDonnell Douglas company, the programme became dogged by reports of technical problems, production delays and cost overruns. Four decades on, the C-17 has overcome these problems and now looks like remaining in service well past 2050.

The origins of the C-17 lie in a far different era, when the US military was bogged down in Southeast Asia and the idea of American troops fighting in Afghanistan would have been considered ludicrous.

In 1972, US Air Force launched a project to replace its Lockheed C-130 Hercules tactical transport with a new jet powered aircraft under the Advanced Medium Short Take-off and Landing Transport (AMST) project. It was only intended to operate close to the frontlines, operating from remote airfields.

Boeing and McDonnell Douglas threw their hats into the AMST ring with rival demonstrator aircraft. The YC-14 was the Boeing offering and it had two jet engines mounted above its wings. McDonnell Douglas came up with the YC-15, which was powered by four underwing jet engines.

By the end of the 1970s, the world had moved on. Tension in the Middle East led the Pentagon to establish the Rapid Deployment Joint Task Force (RDJTF) to be ready to intervene in the volatile region.

The USAF – in partnership with the US Army and US Marine Corps – went back to the drawing board and came up with a completely new requirement. The idea was now to be able to fly up to 62 tons of cargo to the other side of the world and then land on a dirt, austere, airstrip only 914 metres (3,000ft) long.

This was a dramatic recasting of the USAF's airlift ambition and no in-production aircraft matched the performance requirements of what was now known as the C-X Airlift System (Cargo-Experimental) project.

During 1980, the US Air Force worked with American aerospace companies to refine what they wanted from the new aircraft. In October 1980 the final Request for

ABOVE: The McDonnell Douglas YC-15 design was used as the basis for the C-17, proving its revolutionary short take-off and landing technology. USAF

YC-15, which potentially had the performance to undertake all of the C-X mission sets.

On August 28, 1981, McDonnell Douglas was declared the winner of the C-X mission and its Douglas Aircraft Company subsidiary at Long Beach in California began work on the first design that eventually became the C-17. Throughout the 1980s, the Pentagon and rival aircraft manufacturers continued to propose converting airliners to meet part of the C-X solution.

The USAF remained steadfast in supporting the C-17 concept and in December 1985 issued a Full-Scale Development contract worth $3.4 billion, with the intention for the first flight to take place in February 1990 and for a fleet of 210 aircraft to be delivered by 1999.

Two years later work on the first components began and on August 24, 1988, the first prototype, aircraft T-1, started to be assembled inside the Douglas Aircraft Company's giant Long Beach hangar. This building is one of the most iconic in the American aviation industry dating back to 1941 and it would soon be the hub for all C-17 assembly for the next twenty-seven years.

The initial work on the C-17 prototype was far from straightforward and the McDonnell Douglas design team soon ran into technical problems. Its weight rose by 8.2% which threatened to undermine the aircraft's performance. »

Proposals (RFP) was issued by the Pentagon, which resulted in Boeing, Lockheed and McDonnell Douglas putting in solutions.

Boeing offered a modified YC-14 and a cargo-carrying version of the 747 Jumbo Jet. Lockheed came up with a new design based on their existing C-141 Starlifter, as well as a cargo-carrying version of their L1011 Tristar airliner. Both companies were offering a mix of aircraft types to meet the C-X requirements, with the converted airliners flying cargo into an airfield in the forward theatre of operations and then passing this onto airlifters with the capability to land on austere strips.

McDonnell Douglas offered up an advanced version of their

RIGHT: The C-17 prototype T-1 flew for 20 years from Edwards AFB to help develop the aircraft. It is now on display at the National Museum of the USAF in Dayton, Ohio. Boeing

The flight control system suffered problems, and its supplier had to be changed. Supply issues plagued the project and then McDonnell Douglas hit financial troubles, forcing the company to lay off thousands of its skilled workers.

As a result of all these problems, the first flight of T-1 kept being put back and back. It was finally rolled out from Long Beach on December 21, 1990, and took to the skies over Southern California on September 15, 1991.

In the midst of these problems, the Cold War ended after the collapse of the Berlin Wall in November 1989, prompting massive cuts to the Pentagon's budget. This led to a reduction of the order book for the C-17 and a slowing down of production. The in-service date was slipped back to May 1994 for the aircraft which was now officially named the Globemaster III.

The programme continued to be plagued by technical problems and in early 1993 the Pentagon began looking for alternatives. This resulted in the order book for C-17s being cut to just 40 airframes.

To try to turn around this situation, McDonnell Douglas and the USAF joined forces to come up with a new way forward. The company's management was shaken up and the manufacturing process re-structured. Slowly, these reforms began to pay off and by June 1994 deliveries of new aircraft from Long Beach were back on schedule. The USAF's test programme was also starting to gain momentum and in January 1995 the aircraft achieved its initial operational capability target. During 1995 reliability, maintainability and availability (RM&A) trials showed that the aircraft could do what was required of it in a range of demanding tactical scenarios.

With confidence now high that the aircraft was performing well, the Pentagon's procurement board recommend in January 1996 that multi-year contracts for 80 aircraft be placed with McDonnell Douglas and 350 F117-PW-100 engines with Pratt & Whitney. The package was worth $14.2 billion and eventually resulted in a formal contract awarded in May 1996. This put the unit price of the aircraft at $177 million each.

The shake-up of the American aerospace industry caused by the end of the Cold War was still not complete. In August 1997, McDonnell Douglas was taken over by the Boeing Company. America's largest aircraft manufacturer now took charge of a major programme that was moving from a troubled development phase into full scale production. C-17 assembly remained in place at the old Douglas factory

ABOVE: The last C-17, aircraft 10-0223, built for the USAF took off from Long Beach on September 12, 2013. USAF

LEFT: The C-17 prototype T-1 outside the Douglas Aircraft Company plant in Long Beach, where all subsequent C-17s were assembled. Douglas Aircraft Company/ Boeing

in Long Beach, but the aircraft branding changed.

Over the next twelve years production ramped up, with 16 aircraft a year being delivered between 2002 and 2009. Boeing embarked on a major drive to sell the aircraft to foreign air forces and eventually won orders for 53 C-17s from eight air forces. The USAF took delivery of 223 production standard aircraft up to 2013. One aircraft was lost in an accident in 2010.

Efforts to sell the aircraft to civilian cargo operations proved fruitless and by the 2010s the Pentagon said it had enough aircraft, with the last aircraft for the USAF being delivered in 2013. Foreign orders kept the line going for two more years when the last aircraft was completed for Qatar, before being handed over in 2016. The final Indian aircraft was handed over three years later.

In June 2019, Boeing announced that it had finally sold its Long Beach site and its famous hangar for $200 million to an Australian property developer, bringing to an end nearly 80 years of aviation history. »

C-17 programme – significant events of the first two decades

1979
December 10
C-X programme initiated

1980
October 15
Request for Proposal released to industry

1981
August 28
Source Selection Announced, McDonnell Douglas design wins C-X competition

1982
July 23
Full-Scale Engineering Development (FSED) contract awarded to McDonnell Douglas

1985
December 31
C-17 Full Scale Development contract approved

1987
January
Contract for long lead items for Lot I (2 aircraft) awarded

November 2
Fabrication of first part for first aircraft, T-1, begins

1988
August 24
T-1 assembly started

1989
January 28
Milestone IIIA approved, Low-Rate Initial Production decision

October 30
Defense Acquisition Board announces programme restructure

1990
June 30
T-1 goes to final assembly, First production aircraft, P-1, goes to major join of airframe structures

December 21
T-1 final assembly completed

1991
September 15
T-1 first flight

1992
January 17
Flight Test programme surpassed 100 flight hours

May 18
P-1 first flight

1993
June 14
First C-17, aircraft P-6, entered USAF operational service

November 22
First live personnel static line airdrops

1994
January 6
C-17 'Omnibus Settlement' agreement to start full rate production

June 3
C-17 sets short take-off and landing world record

September 28
Heavy equipment airdrop loads tested to 60,000 lbs

October 14
First operational C-17 mission

1995
January 17
C-17 initial operating capability declared

February 14
C-17 fleet surpassed 10,000 flying hours

February 15
C-17 awarded the Collier Aviation Trophy

1996
May
US Congress approved multi-year purchase of 80 C-17s

1998
December
C-17 operational fleet reached 100,000 flying hours

For 25 years C-17s were assembled at Long Beach in southern California. Boeing

C-17 DESCRIBED

A Walk Around

RIGHT: C-17 pilots monitor the aircraft systems on multi-function displays and use head-up displays during tactical landings. USAF

Nothing quite looks like the Boeing C-17A Globemaster III. It's big, wide and heavy. Yet, it is also nimble in the air and a quick mover on the ground.

Once design work began in the late 1970s, the USAF and McDonnell Douglas were keen to develop an aircraft that could replace the old Lockheed C-141 Starlifter. It also took on some of the missions flown by the big Lockheed C-5 Galaxy strategic airlifter and its little brother, the tactical Lockheed C-130 Hercules.

Not surprisingly, the C-17's design was centred around its cargo hold and a large tail ramp so vehicles could drive directly into the aircraft without needing any sort of assistance or cargo handling equipment. This requirement drove the C-17's designers to adopt high

BELOW: The iconic C-17 prototype, T-1, on a test flight over California. USAF

ABOVE: The C-17s unique short take-off and landing capabilities have been demonstrated repeatedly on trials and live operations around the world. USAF

wing configuration to make the cargo hold work better.

The C-17's design originated in the 1970s, when the McDonnell Douglas YC-15 demonstrators took to the skies. This crucially proved the short take-off and landing (STOL) characteristics that were eventually incorporated into the C-17. A new engine, which were eventually designated the Pratt & Whitney F117-PW-100 turbo fans, were developed for the YC-15. They were subsequently installed in the C-17 and the Boeing 757 family of airliners.

Every C-17 built was assembled inside the giant Long Beach hangar that dates back to the days of the Douglas Aircraft Company in World War Two. Fittingly, thousands of the classic Douglas DC-3/C-47 Dakota/Skytrain airlifters were built in the hangar.

Assembly of C-17s began with the fabrication of the fuselage from a series of ribs and longerons. Once the main fuselage took shape, the wings and cantilever T-typed »

RIGHT: C-17s are operated by a three-person crew, with the loadmaster having his own jump seat in the aircraft's cockpit. USAF

ABOVE: Crew and passengers usually enter the aircraft through its front cabin door. USAF

BELOW: Many C-17s are protected by AN/AAQ-24 Large Aircraft Infrared Countermeasures (LAIRCM) to allow them to operate in high threat regions. USAF

Passenger carrying options start with the basic side seats, with 27 folding Kevlar seats positioned along the side of the cargo hold. The aircraft crew can rapidly install 48 temporary seats in the centre of the fuselage to allow 102 paratroopers to be carried.

For long distance missions, the cargo hold can be reconfigured with pallet-based airliner style-passenger seats to allow 188 passengers to be carried. Part of this package is a comfort pallet containing an additional toilet and an extra galley to prepare hot food and drinks.

Medical evacuation is a very important mission, with 36 litter/stretcher stations kits to be installed in the cargo hold. Up to 102 walking wounded and medical staff can be carried in addition to the serious casualties on litters.

In extreme situations, where passenger comfort is not a priority. Hundreds of passengers can be accommodated on the cargo hold floor, with temporary straps securing

tail were attached. The majority of the material used was aluminium, which makes up 69.3% of the aircraft's structures, with remainder comprising 12.3% steel, 10.3% titanium and 8.1% composite materials.

Over time, the design of the aircraft's structure has evolved, with the all-metal stabiliser being replaced from airframe 51 with a hybrid metal/composite one, which is 20% lighter than on earlier aircraft.

The C-17 is designed to allow its crew to carry up to 65 tons of cargo over strategic distances and still be able to land and take off from austere or unprepared airstrips.

To achieve this mission, the cargo hold of the C-17 is specifically designed to allow the rapid loading and unloading of out-sized cargo.

The rear ramp allows the vehicles, including up to a M1A1 Abrams main battle tank, to drive directly up into the C-17s hold. Loadmasters

then secure vehicles to many of the 295 cargo-tie down rings, spread around the hold. Once at a forward airstrip, the ramp is opened, and vehicles can drive straight off and head into action.

There are a number of cargo carrying options. Large cargo pallets can be carried, which can be loaded by a forklift or a flatbed loading vehicle. A system of rails and rollers means pallets can be pulled inside the cargo hold via a hoist, controlled by the loadmaster from his station next to the rear ramp.

The C-17's cargo handling system can be adapted to allow for pallets or containers to be parachuted out of the rear ramp. An extraction system, again operated by the loadmaster, pulls out the pallets and containers by opening a first drogue parachute. This then pulls out the rest of the pallets in a matter of seconds and activates the main parachutes.

RIGHT: Loadmasters tie down cargo in a C-17s hold using an array of securing points. USAF

BELOW: Large-outsized cargo, such as AH-64 attack helicopters are routinely carried in C-17s. USAF

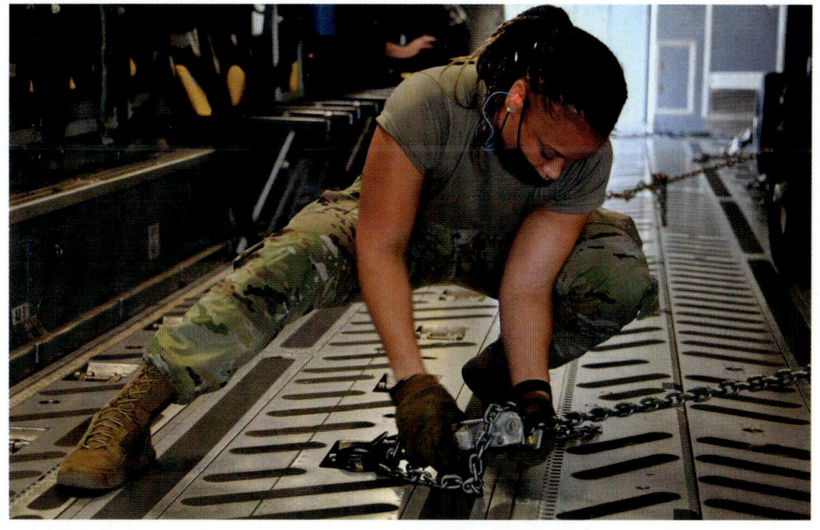

passengers during take-off, landing or turbulence.

To deliver paratroopers, static line equipment can be fitted in the cargo hold, along with the red light/green light warning lights to allow jumpmasters to control the tactical parachute jumps from rear-side doors. High-altitude low-opening (HALO) jumps by Special Forces operatives can be made off an open rear ramp.

To allow the flight crew to rest during long distance missions, there are two bunks and additional seating in a rest area behind the flight deck. This means a 'slip' flight deck crew can be carried, who are able to be rested and ready to take over flying the aircraft after prolonged periods. Below the rest area is a galley and toilet to help with crew comfort.

The provision of crew facilities is vital because of the long distances involved in many C-17 missions, which can be extended dramatically by the use of air-to-air refuelling. In 1998, this global reach was demonstrated in a 19 hour-long mission to drop paratroopers into Central Asia during a training exercise.

The C-17 was designed from the start to operate from rough or austere airstrips, where there is minimal or no cargo handling equipment available. In such scenarios, vehicles can drive straight off the rear ramp, or a forklift can be carried, which drives off the aircraft and »

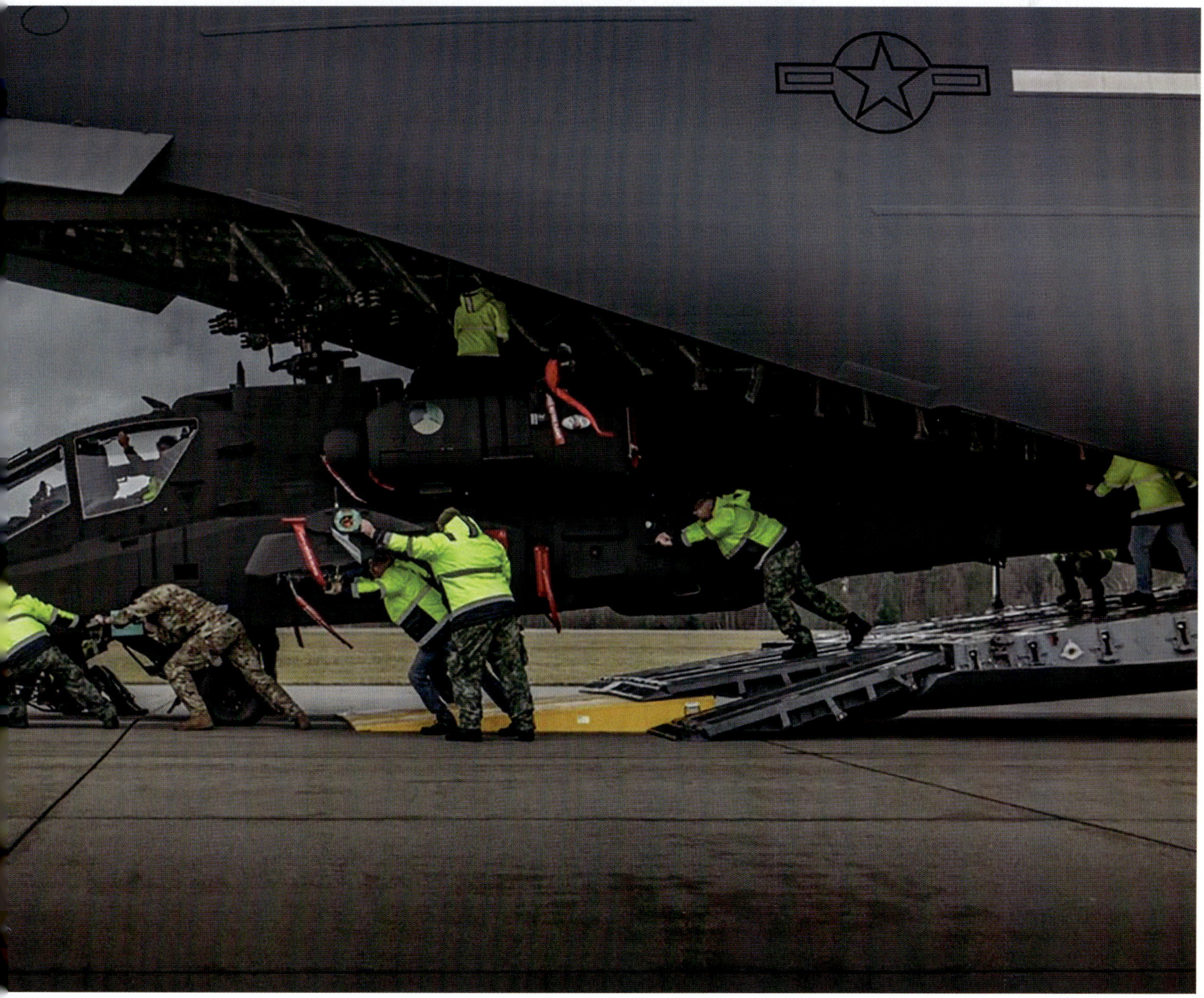

then begins to move pallets off the rear ramp.

An auxiliary power unit (APU) is installed in the starboard main landing gear pod, to allow the aircraft to be started without any external APU. To allow the aircraft to be manoeuvred on congested airstrips, it can make a 180 degree 'U'-turn in 24 metres.

To help the pilots land on small strips in bad weather, the flight deck has two head-up-displays (HUD), which provide primary flight data and steering cues. These HUDs are similar to those used in fighter jets, and they allow the pilots to give all their attention to looking out of cockpit windows during approaches in busy and complex tactical situations.

The C-17 incorporated a fully digital fly-by-wire flight control systems and the flight information

ABOVE: Tactical parachuting of airborne troops and cargo pallets is a core mission of the C-17. USAF

LEFT: Cargo pallets can be rapidly loaded onto to C-17s using USAF K-loaders. USAF

RIGHT: C-17 loadmasters control the aircraft's automated loading systems from a single console at the rear of cargo hold. USAF

BELOW: Tactical seating can be installed in the C-17s hold to allow paratroopers and soldiers be seated for long range missions. USAF

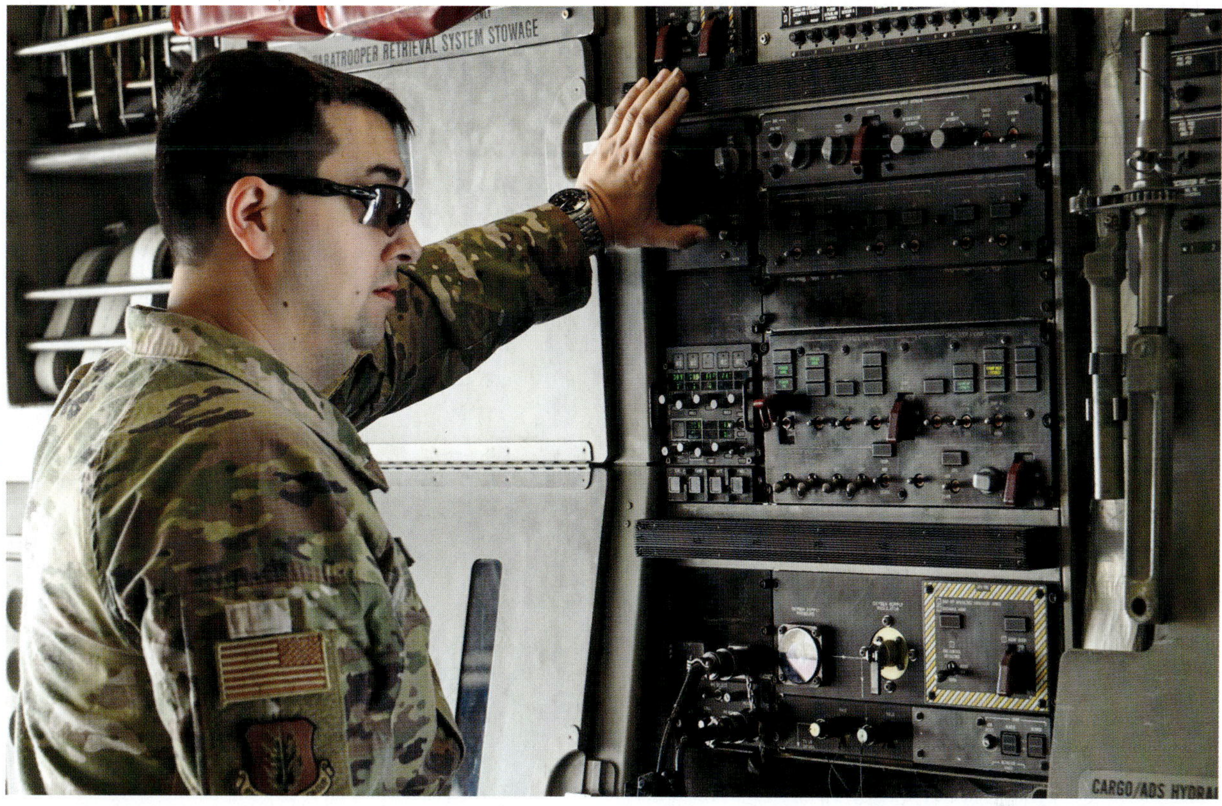

is displayed in six computer screens, making it one of the first 'glass cockpit' aircraft to enter USAF service.

The key to the C-17s ability to get in and out of small strips, is the aircraft's big flaps, which are designed to help bring the aircraft rapidly to a halt and take off in short distances. According to Boeing, this allows a C-17 to land on 915 metres of runway. Thrust reversers fitted to the aircraft F117-PW-100 engines allows a fully loaded C-17 to reverse up a 2-degree slope.

To protect the C-17 during low level operations in high threat regions, the aircraft is fitted with a range of defensive systems, depending on mission requirements.

The core C-17 defensive aid suite is based on a AN/AAR-47 missile approach warning system (MAWS) that alerts the flight deck crew to approaching enemy surface-to-air »

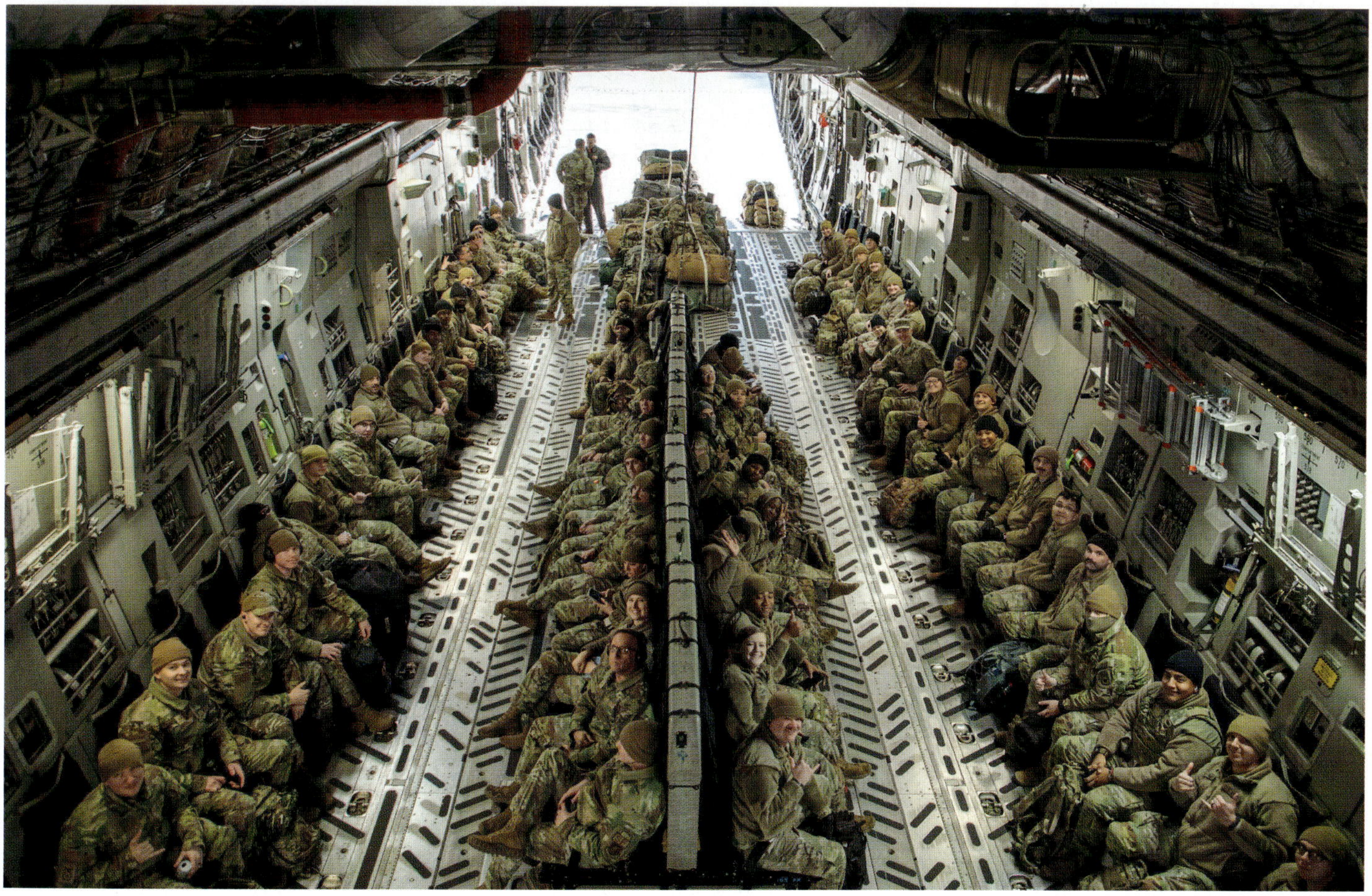

ABOVE: A USAF engineer performs maintenance on a C-17s AN/AAR-47 missile approach warning system (MAWS) at McChord AFB. USAF

missiles (SAMs). This detects the hot exhaust of the missile, which allows countermeasures from the AN/ALE-47 dispensing pods positioned around the airframe to be deployed. These are a mix of flares to decoy heat seeking SAMs or foil chaff to confuse radar guided weapons.

Every C-17 is fitted with this basic level defensive equipment but from 2003, the first of 79 aircraft were fitted a higher level of protection. This includes the AN/AAQ-24 Large Aircraft Infrared Countermeasures (LAIRCM) system, which is mounted in turrets around the fuselage C-17s. The LAIRCM has a detector and a powerful laser that 'burns out' the seeker head of heatseeking missiles. When set in fully automatic mode, the LAIRCM is credited with being able to neutralise in-bound missiles in only a few seconds.

Each aircraft is fitted with a satellite communications system to allow Air Mobility Command headquarters at Scott Air Force Base in Illinois direct global C-17 operations.

To enable C-17s to conduct mass troop parachute and cargo drops, the aircraft are fitted with specialist avionics equipment. A Formation Flight System allows a formation of 53 C-17s to be flown across drop zones in 30 minutes to drop a brigade-sized contingent of paratroopers, as well as cargo pallets.

RIGHT: Air-to-air refuelling gives the C-17 global reach but requires regular training to maintain crew proficiency in the demanding skills required for this technique. USAF

This equipment also includes a mid-airborne collision avoidance system – formation rendezvous system (MILACAS-FR) which enables 99 aircraft to fly in close proximity in zero visibility conditions.

Although externally every C-17 looks similar, through the life of the aircraft the internal configurations and capabilities have been updated. A lot of these modifications were carried out to help reduce manufacturing time and costs.

Modifications were installed in C-17s in a series of 'blocks' and they generally matched the 'production lots' or contracts let by the US Department of Defense.

The most important block upgrades are as follows:

- Block 1 to 8
  Prototype aircraft were brought up to production configuration. From aircraft 32 onwards, redesigned and strengthened wings were incorporated and from aircraft 51 composite tailplane and improved avionics were added.
- Block 9
  Improved production version from aircraft 71, with a larger centre section wing fuel tank for extend range, upgraded software and redesigned cockpit displays. For a time, these aircraft were also known aa C-17ERs.
- Block 11
  These featured automatic pressurisation and depressurisation; aircrew data transfer device, including automatic upload of worldwide navigational data, maintenance date and loadmaster software; chest-mounted oxygen regulator to allow loadmaster to move about the cabin during high-altitude airdrops; and electrical improvement project, that rewired the aircraft to make it easier and less costly to produce.
- Block 13
  Terrain Awareness Warning System, a reactive wind-shear warning system to improve the performance of the (MILACAS-FR) and follow-on improvements to various computer systems that enhance the aircraft's mission capability and safety.
- Block 14
  Replacement weather radar, a redesigned stabiliser strut and secure communication enhancement.
- Block 15
  Upgraded on-board inert gas generating system along with navigation and safety modifications.

- Block 16
  Avionics modernisation package and a weather radar modification, fuel system retrofit, improved stabiliser strut system, main landing gear deficiency corrections, including a wheel brake and tire cost saving initiative.
- Block 17
  This was a major enhancement, which included a local area network to allow army commanders on aircraft to conduct planning with colleagues on other aircraft en route to combat missions. Protection against 12.7mm rounds for the liquid oxygen bottles, combat lighting in the main cabin and Required Navigation Performance – Improvement (RNP-I) upgrade fitted.
- Block 21
  New hardware and software for the Automatic Dependent Surveillance-Broadcast Out (ADS-B Out) system required by the US Federal Aviation Administration and aviation authorities in Europe for planes operating in controlled airspace. This is a next generation transponder system which broadcasts the precise position and location information of an aircraft in real time, giving air traffic control better visibility to track and manage aircraft while enhancing aircraft safety by providing aircrew more situational awareness of nearby aircraft. In addition to ADS-B Out, the upgrade included an Identification of Friend or Foe (IFF) modification and other communication/navigation capability software updates. These additional modifications significantly improve the aircraft's flight management systems.

Since the closure of the Boeing Long Beach assembly in 2015, these upgrades are now incorporated on in-service aircraft as they are rotated through their planned maintenance overhauls at USAF bases, where they were generally brought up to the latest configuration. This ensures the fleet remains in a common configuration, which in turn ensured the long-term costs of ownership are reduced so fewer types of spare parts are needed. Non-US C-17 operators have routinely updated their aircraft in line with the USAF.

The C-17 has proved to be a robust and reliable aircraft. Since it entered service, only one has been lost in a serious accident during an air display in 2010 that resulted in four fatalities and loss of the aircraft. An investigation attributed the crash to pilot error, rather than any technical issue with the aircraft.

BOEING C-17A GLOBEMASTER III TECHNICAL SPECIFICATIONS

General characteristics

Length	53m (174ft)
Wingspan	51.755m (169ft 9.6in)
Height	6.79m (55ft 1in)
Empty weight	128,140kg (282,500lb)
Max take-off weight	265,352kg (585,000lb)
Powerplant	4 × Pratt & Whitney PW2000 turbofan engines (US military designation: F117-PW-100)

Performance

Cruise speed	830 km/h (520 mph)
Range (without air-to-air refuelling)	4,480 km (2,780 miles) with 157,000 lb (71,214 kg) payload
Ferry range	11,540km (7,170miles)
Service ceiling	4,000m (45,000ft)
Take-off run at MTOW	2,499m (8,200ft)
Take-off run at 179,169 kg (395,000lb)	3,000ft (914m)
Landing distance	1,067m (3,500ft)

Avionics

AlliedSignal AN/APS-133(V) weather and mapping radar	

Capacity

Crew	3 (2 pilots, 1 loadmaster) 102 paratroopers or 134 troops with palletised and sidewall seats or 54 troops with sidewall seats only or 36 litter and 54 ambulatory patients and medical attendants
Capacity	77,519 kg (170,900 lb) of cargo distributed at max over 18 463L master pallets or a mix of palletised cargo and vehicles
Vehicle Cargo	one M1 Abrams tank, two Bradley armoured vehicles, or three Stryker armoured vehicles

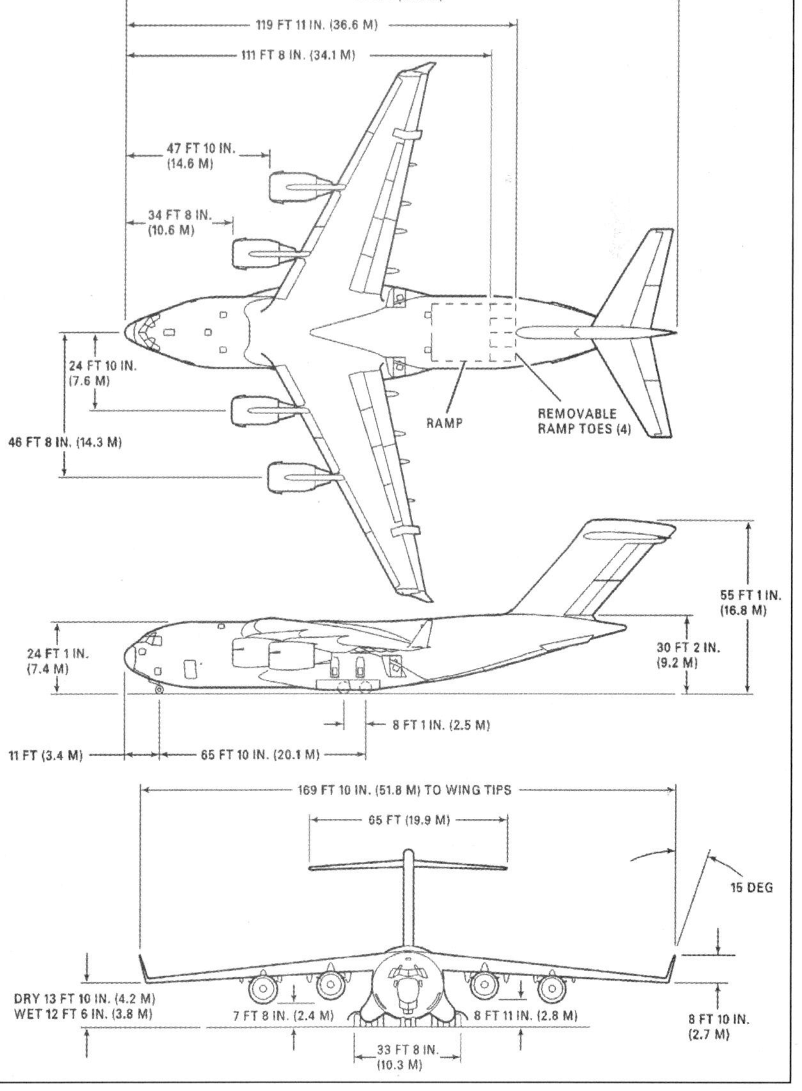

TRAINING TO FLY THE C-17

Achieving the Airlift Mission

ABOVE: Altus AFB is home to all USAF C-17 aircrew conversion training. USAF

RIGHT: C-17 loadmasters are an integral part of C-17 crews and are trained alongside pilots at Altus AFB. USAF

Flying the Boeing C-17A Globemaster III is like no other airlift aircraft. When it entered service in the mid-1990s, the C-17 broke new ground for airlift aviators.

The most revolutionary aspect of the aircraft was the move to a two-crew cockpit and a single loadmaster in the cargo hold. By introducing 'glass cockpit' technology there was no need for a flight engineer. Automated cargo handling technology allowed a single loadmaster to do the work of two or three people.

Despite all this new technology, C-17 crews still need to work as a team to achieve their mission and from the start of their training they

have to understand how to get the best of their aircraft and crewmates.

The 97th Operations Group is the home of the Air Force's only KC-135, KC-46, and C-17 formal training units (FTU), responsible for initial and upgrade aircrew training for all three weapons systems. Its elite instructor corps provides training in specialised areas including aerial refuelling, airdrop, night vision goggle operations, low-level environments, assault zone landings, as well as tactical procedures.

On January 30, 1996, the 58th Airlift Squadron was activated as part of the 97th Air Mobility Wing at Altus Air Force base in Oklahoma. Under the Air Education and Training Command, the 58th Airlift Squadron is responsible for the formal flight training of all C-17 pilots and loadmasters, as well as maintaining worldwide readiness in case of contingencies requiring highly experienced aircrews.

The 58th Airlift Squadron has participated in the longest airdrop mission in history, from Pope Air Force Base in North Carolina to Kazakhstan, in the former Soviet Union. It provided critical airlift to Europe during the conflict in Kosovo.

For C-17 student training, the initial qualification curriculum consists of three different phases. The first phase is learning technical instructions through Computer Based Training (CBT), which focuses on providing the foundational knowledge of aircraft systems, normal and emergency procedures, and operating limitations that the aircrew need to successfully operate the C-17.

Next is practicing and applying knowledge through simulators, which provides a safe and economical way for students to gain practical hands-on understanding of the various academic topics, aircraft operating procedures, and gain basic C-17 qualification. Finally, once all their learning objectives are completed, students get to progress to the flight-line where they operate the aircraft and gain their basic mission employment qualification.

Before operating simulators, initial qualification students solely dedicate their time to studying using CBT. The initial stage of training is for students to familiarise themselves with all the specific aspects of the C-17 before applying their skills in a controlled environment.

Student C-17 loadmasters and pilots have to undergo around 300 CBTs and 700 simulator lessons in total.

Loadmaster students get to train on a Cargo Compartment Trainer, which is identical to the C-17 with all the vital aspects including switches and panels, excluding the loadmaster's station.

Part of being a loadmaster is directing cargo loading, learning how to take charge, and building confidence, which requires hands on training. The students go through about 14 different qualification lessons to ensure they are ready for the day they get to step on the actual aircraft."

C-17 pilots get their preflight hands-on training utilising a single simulator based on the cockpit of the aircraft.

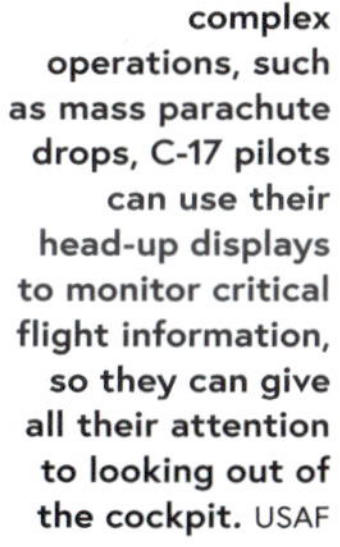

BY THE NUMBERS

The USAF C-17 Fleet

Constructor's Number	US DoD Serials	Prototypes/ Pre-Production	Lot	Markings/Notes
50002	87-0025	YC-17A/T-1		Now on display at National Musuem of USAF
50003		Static test		
50004		Static test		
50005	88-0265	P-1	I	
50006	88-0266	P-2	I	
50007	89-1189	P-3	II	
50008	89-1190	P-4	II	
50009	89-1191	P-5	II	
50010	89-1192	P-6	II	Spirit of Charleston
50011	90-0532	P -7	III	
50012	90-0533		III	
50013	90-0534		III	
50014	90-0535		III	
50015	92-3291		IV	
50016	92-3292		IV	D-Day Invasion Stripes applied
50017	92-3293		IV	
50018	92-3294		IV	
50019	93-0599		V	
50020	93-0600		V	
50021	93-0601		V	
50022	93-0602		V	City of Altus
50023	93-0603		V	
50024	93-0604		V	
50025	94-0065		VI	
50026	94-0066		VI	
50027	94-0067		VI	
50028	94-0068		VI	The Spirit of Airborne
50029	94-0069		VI	
50030	94-0070		VI	
50031	95-0102		VII	
50032	95-0103		VII	
50033	95-0104		VII	
50034	95-0105		VII	
50035	95-0106		VII	
50036	95-0107		VII	
50037	96-0001		VIII	
50038	96-0002		VIII	Spirit of the Air Force
50039	96-0003		VIII	
50040	96-0004		VIII	
50041	96-0005		VIII	The Spirit of Sgt. John L. Levitow
50042	96-0006		VIII	The Spirit of Berlin
50043	96-0007		VIII	The Spirit of America's Veterans
50044	96-0008		VIII	Spirit of the Total Force
50045	97-0041		IX	
50046	97-0042		IX	Spirit of Tuskegee Airmen
50047	97-0043		IX	Spirit of Los Angeles
50048	97-0044		IX	Spirit of Fairborn
50049	97-0045		IX	
50050	97-0046		IX	
50051	97-0047		IX	Spirit of Middle Georgia
50052	97-0048		IX	
50053	98-0049		X	
50054	98-0050		X	
50055	98-0051		X	
50056	98-0052		X	Spirit of McChord
50057	98-0053		X	
50058	98-0054		X	
50059	98-0055		X	
50060	98-0056		X	

Constructor's Number	US DoD Serials	Prototypes/ Pre-Production	Lot	Markings/Notes
50061	98-0057		XI	
50062	99-0058		XI	
50063	99-0059		XI	
50064	99-0060		XI	
50065	99-0061		XI	
50066	99-0062		XI	Spirit of the Hump
50067	99-0063		XI	Spirit of the Wright Brothers
50068	99-0064		XI	City of St. Louis
50069	99-0165		XI	
50070	99-0166		XI	
50071	99-0167		XI	
50072	99-0168		XI	
50073	99-0169		XI	
50074	99-0170		XI	
50075	00-0171		XII	
50076	00-0172		XII	Spirit of the Cascades
50077	00-0173		XII	Spirit of the Aleutians/ Lost 28/7/2010
50080	00-0174		XII	Spirit of the Sourdoughs
50083	00-0175		XII	Spirit of Connecticut
50084	00-0176		XII	
50085	00-0177		XII	
50086	00-0178		XII	
50087	00-0179		XII	
50088	00-0180		XII	
50089	00-0181		XII	
50090	00-0182		XII	
50091	00-0183		XII	
50092	00-0184		XII	
50093	00-0185		XII	The American Spirit
50094	01-0186		XIII	
50095	01-0187		XIII	
50096	01-0188		XIII	
50097	01-0189		XIII	
50098	01-0190		XIII	
50099	01-0191		XIII	
50100	01-0192		XIII	
50101	01-0193		XIII	Spirit of Strom Thurmond
50102	01-0194		XIII	
50103	01-0195		XIII	
50104	01-0196		XIII	
50105	01-0197		XIII	
50106	02-1098		XIV	
50107	02-1099		XIV	
50108	02-1100		XIV	
50109	02-1101		XIV	
50110	02-1102		XIV	
50111	02-1103		XIV	

ABOVE: The USAF currently operates a fleet of 222 Boeing C-17A Globemaster aircraft. Several have been named in honour of their home states, prominent local figures, or historic links to the USAF. USAF

Constructor's Number	US DoD Serials	Prototypes/ Pre-Production	Lot	Markings/Notes
50112	02-1104		XIV	
50113	02-1105		XIV	
50114	02-1106		XIV	
50115	02-1107		XIV	
50116	02-1108		XIV	
50117	02-1109		XIV	
50118	02-1110		XIV	
50119	02-1111		XIV	
50120	02-1112		XIV	The Spirit of the Mississippi Minutemen
50121	03-3113		XV-A	Spirit of the Purple Heart
50122	03-3114		XV-A	
50123	03-3115		XV-A	
50124	03-3116		XV-A	
50125	03-3117		XV-A	
50126	03-3118		XV-A	
50127	03-3119		XV-A	Spirit of G.V. "Sonny" Montgomery
50128	03-3120		XV-A	
50129	03-3121		XV-B	
50130	03-3122		XV-B	
50131	03-3123		XV-B	
50132	03-3124		XV-B	
50133	03-3125		XV-B	Spirit of New Jersey
50134	03-3126		XV-B	
50135	03-3127		XV-B	
50136	04-4128		XVI	
50137	04-4129		XVI	
50138	04-4130		XVI	
50139	04-4131		XVI	Spirit of Thomas B. McGuire
50140	04-4132		XVI	
50141	04-4133		XVI	
50142	04-4134		XVI	
50143	04-4135		XVI	
50144	04-4136		XVI	
50145	04-4137		XVI	
50146	04-4138		XVI	Spirit of California
50147	05-5139		XVII	
50148	05-5140		XVII	
50149	05-5141		XVII	
50150	05-5142		XVII	
50151	05-5143		XVII	
50152	05-5144		XVII	Spirit of Rosie the Riveter
50153	05-5145		XVII	Spirit of Ronald Reagan
50154	05-5146		XVII	Spirit of Hawai'i – Ke Aloha
50155	05-5147		XVII	Spirit of Daniel Inouye
50156	05-5148		XVII	
50157	05-5149		XVII	
50158	05-5150		XVII	
50159	05-5151		XVII	
50160	05-5152		XVII	Spirit of 'Go for Broke'
50161	05-5153		XVII	Spirit of Kamehameha-Imua
50162	06-6154		XVIII	Spirit of Solano W

Constructor's Number	US DoD Serials	Prototypes/ Pre-Production	Lot	Markings/Notes
50163	06-6155		XVIII	Spirit of Benicia
50164	06-6156		XVIII	Spirit of the Golden Bear
50165	06-6157		XVIII	
50166	06-6158		XVIII	
50168	06-6159		XVIII	Spirit of Golden Gate
50169	06-6160		XVIII	Spirit of Rio Vista W
50170	06-6161		XVIII	
50171	06-6162		XVIII	
50172	06-6163		XVIII	
50173	06-6164		XVIII	Spirit of Vallejo
50175	06-6165		XVIII	Spirit of Constitution
50176	06-6166		XVIII	
50177	06-6167		XVIII	
50179	06-6168		XVIII	
50180	07-7169		XIX	
50182	07-7170		XIX	
50183	07-7171		XIX	
50189	07-7172		XIX	
50190	07-7173		XIX	
50192	07-7174		XIX	
50193	07-7175		XIX	
50194	07-7176		XIX	
50195	07-7177		XIX	
50196	07-7178		XIX	Spirit of Delaware
50197	07-7179		XIX	Spirit of Travis
50198	07-7180		XIX	
50199	07-7181		XIX	
50200	07-7182		XIX	
50201	07-7183		XIX	
50202	07-7184		XIX	
50203	07-7185		XIX	
50204	07-7186		XIX	
50205	07-7187		XIX	
50206	07-7188		XIX	
50207	08-7189		XIX	
50213	08-8190		XIX	
50214	08-8191		XX	
50215	08-8192		XX	
50216	08-8193		XX	
50217	08-8194		XX	
50218	08-8195		XX	
50219	08-8196		XX	
50220	08-8197		XX	
50221	08-8198		XX	
50222	08-8199		XX	
50223	08-8200		XX	
50224	08-8201		XX	
50225	08-8202		XX	
50226	08-8203		XX	
50227	08-8204		XX	
50229	09-9205		XX	
50230	09-9206		XXI	
50231	09-/9207		XXI	
50232	09-9208		XXI	
50233	09-9209		XXI	
50234	09-9210		XXI	
50237	09-9211		XXI	
50241	09-9212		XXI	
50242	10-0213		XXI	
50243	10-0214		XXII	
50244	10-0215		XXII	
50245	10-0216		XXII	
50249	10-0217		XXII	
50250	10-0218		XXII	
50255	10-0219		XXII	
50256	10-0220		XXII	
50257	10-0221		XXII	
50258	10-0222		XXII	
50261	10-0223		XXII	

ABOVE: C-17 serial 02-1103 was ordered in 2002, as part of production Lot XIV and it was subsequently assigned to the 446th Airlift Wing at McChord AFB in Washington State. USAF

ABOVE: Planned/Scheduled Depot Level Maintenance (P/SDLM) of C-17s takes place at the Warner Robins Air Logistics Complex at Robins AFB in Georgia. USAF

KEEPING THE C-17 FLYING

Sustaining the Globemaster Fleet

RIGHT: A joint team of USAF, DoD civilians and industry contractors work on the C-17 sustainment programme. USAF

Keeping the global fleet of Boeing C-17A Globemaster IIIs flying is the responsibility of Boeing and the US Air Force, who jointly operate a network of maintenance and repair facilities.

Once production of new airframes ended in 2015, Boeing and the USAF's Air Material Command (AMC) had to work to husband the C-17 fleet to ensure it remained fully operational as long as possible. Regular maintenance and investment in keeping the supply chain for spare parts fully functioning was essential to ensure that the current global 275-strong fleet of C-17s were kept in flyable condition out beyond 2040 and maybe into the 2050s.

For aircraft that are so heavily used in very demanding environments, this is a major challenge. The key to this is ensuring that preventative maintenance activities, including regular overhauls, take place on schedule, to keep aircraft in peak condition.

After the 2021 Kabul evacuation operation, a major maintenance effort was mounted to inspect and repair aircraft that were involved in the demanding mission.

Just as important, are efforts to ensure the supply chain for spare parts remains active so a series of long-term contracts have been placed to keep suppliers of key components in business. Design and engineering teams are also retained by Boeing and AMC to ensure the necessary expertise is available to work on the aircraft.

With an out of service date predicted for the late 2040s and possibly into the 2050s, consideration is also being given to long term upgrade plans including re-sparing wings, new engines, improved avionics and enhanced cockpit systems. This is at an early stage but serious consideration will have to be given to these proposals in the 2030s.

From the start of its service in the USAF, Boeing has been closely involved in the sustainment and support of the C-17 fleet under a series of performance-based logistics (PBL) contracts. When the aircraft started to be delivered to

RIGHT: Modern technology is used to monitor the health of C-17 airframe as they undergo maintenance. USAF

BELOW: C-17s are stripped down to their bare metal and almost all components, including engines are removed during major depot level maintenance. USAF

international customers, they were brought under the umbrella of the Boeing contracts with the USAF.

The C-17 sustainment model is unique to the aircraft, which sees Boeing holding an overarching support contract but maintenance and repair work on aircraft is carried out at operator's facilities around the world.

Boeing's work on the C-17 fleet is funded via a series of three-to-four year-long 'block' contracts for engineering, field support, and material management, for the global fleet of 275 aircraft. This allows work requirements to be adjusted, with the $3.5 billion contract in 2021 providing additional funding for new work scope such as international staffing to augment maintenance efforts and cyber security.

While sustainment costs typically rise as a fleet ages, Boeing has aimed to lower operating cost per-flight-hour for the global fleet.

"We are bending the cost curve on platforms like the C-17 by leveraging the breadth and depth of Boeing's services capabilities and expertise worldwide, and by applying digital tools and analytics to drive predictability and performance into every C-17 mission," said Dan Gillian, vice president & general manager of US Government Services for Boeing Global Services, in September 2021. "Working in partnership with our military customers, we are deriving data insight from these aircraft that is improving readiness and increasing fleet efficiency," Gillian added. "Analytical insights provide actionable intelligence to predict component failures, troubleshoot errors with greater speed and accuracy, complete repairs faster, and support aircrew decision making."

In March 2025, the US Department of Defense awarded Boeing a further $2.46 billion contract modification to support continued sustainment of the C-17 Globemaster III fleet. This extends work through October 31, 2027, and includes funding from both US and international operators.

According to a Pentagon contract announcement, the sustainment work is to be carried out at multiple US »

locations, including San Antonio, Texas; Robins AFB Base, Georgia; Charleston AFB in South Carolina; and McChord AFB in Washington, along with other domestic and overseas sites.

The Air Force Lifecycle Management Center at Robins AFB is managing the contract, which includes $376.1 million to be spent in 2025 on supporting USAF aircraft and $97.1 million on support for international operators.

At the centre of this support network is Warner Robins Air Logistics Complex at Robins AFB, where Planned/Scheduled Depot Level Maintenance (P/SDLM) takes places. This is where aircraft are stripped down for full overhauls before being returned to service. More routine and flight line maintenance is carried out on frontline airfields by a mix of military, government civilian and industry contractors.

In 2001, the Warner Robins Air Logistics Complex partnered with the Boeing Company to provide P/SDLM. The 402nd Aircraft Maintenance Group and its 562nd Aircraft Maintenance Squadron (AMXS) play a key role in this work.

"The 562nd AMXS operates in a partnership environment with The Boeing Company," said Jonathan Tucker, 562nd AMXS deputy director

ABOVE: The USAF and international C-17 fleet is regularly rotated through Robins AFB to undergo long term scheduled maintenance to ensure that the aircraft can remain in service for as long as possible. USAF

LEFT: The Warner Robins Air Logistics Complex is equipped with specialist equipment to allow C-17s to be disassembled for long term scheduled maintenance. USAF

"The scheduled process of depot maintenance consists of carefully planned steps to receive the aircraft for maintenance, inspect it to determine what needs to be repaired, perform the repairs and operations checks before painting it and returning it to the home station," he said. "The planned processes can be done in as little as 12 days but could also take over six months, depending on the customer's requests and aircraft's condition."

Aircraft can be put through four cycles of maintenance based on the age and configuration of the individual airframe.

"Heavy maintenance is the majority of the workload," said Tucker. "It is performed on the aircraft every six years. Analytical condition inspections are the same, just more of a deeper look at the condition of the airplane for further analysis, and the landing gear gets replaced every 15 years."

"I am constantly inspired by those around me that know so much, work hard without making excuses, and prioritize our squadron's mission week in and week out," he said. "Their commitment is very important as C-17s are relied on today more than ever."

BOTTOM: The USAF hopes its Planned/Scheduled Depot Level Maintenance programme will keep its C-17s in the air out beyond 2050. USAF

BELOW: Testing and repair of the C-17s complex electronic systems is an important part of the long term scheduled maintenance process. USAF

in 2022. "The Boeing Company is the product support integrator, and our squadron is contracted to accomplish inspection, modification, maintenance and repair on the C-17 Globemaster."

"Our mission is to provide both P/SDLM and unscheduled depot level maintenance requirements as well as selected modifications and field team support for C-17 Globemaster aircraft around the world," said Tucker. "Since 2001, the 562nd AMXS has provided exceptional warfighter support by delivering quality depot maintenance on time and on cost and to improve support through continuous process improvement, resulting in reduced costs, increased capacity, maintenance standardization and compliance."

Tucker said the flow of the aircraft is highly scripted, managed and executed to keep flow days down and aircraft availability high.

FLYING THE SECEF

Special Mission C-17s

RIGHT: US Defence Secretary Pete Hegseth is the latest Pentagon chief to use the facilities of the Silver Bullet to direct American military operations.
Pete Hegseth

BELOW: Airmen from the 89th Aerial Port Squadron load a Silver Bullet into a C-17 Globemaster III at Joint Base Andrews outside Washington DC.
USAF

Air Force One is perhaps the most famous US military aircraft, thanks to its high-profile missions flying US Presidents around the world. Its luxurious interior and hi-tech communications turn it into what is sometimes dubbed 'The Flying White House'.

Other senior US political and military leaders need to move long distances by air and keep in communications with the outside world, so they have to be provided with their own flying command posts.

The impressive range, endurance, cargo carrying capacity, and short take-off and landing (STOL) performance of the Boeing C-17A Globemaster III make it very attractive for this role. However, there are some major problems. The aircraft's hold is noisy, and its seating arrangements are far from being anywhere near airliner standard. It is just not possible for VIP passengers, as well as their senior staff and advisors, to work and travel in comfort inside the hold of a C-17.

To get over this problem, in 1991 the US Air Force Research Laboratory developed the 'Silver Bullet' to provide a roll-on, roll-off VIP travel pod for specially configured military transport aircraft. It was originally intended for use on the Lockheed C-5 Galaxy or McDonnell Douglas KC-10 Extender but now is almost exclusively used on C-17s.

The solution involved the modification of a commercial travel trailer (caravan to Europeans) to enable it to be rapidly loaded into the cargo hold of a C-17 and then connected to power and communications cabling. The iconic American company, Airstream, were chosen to provide the travel

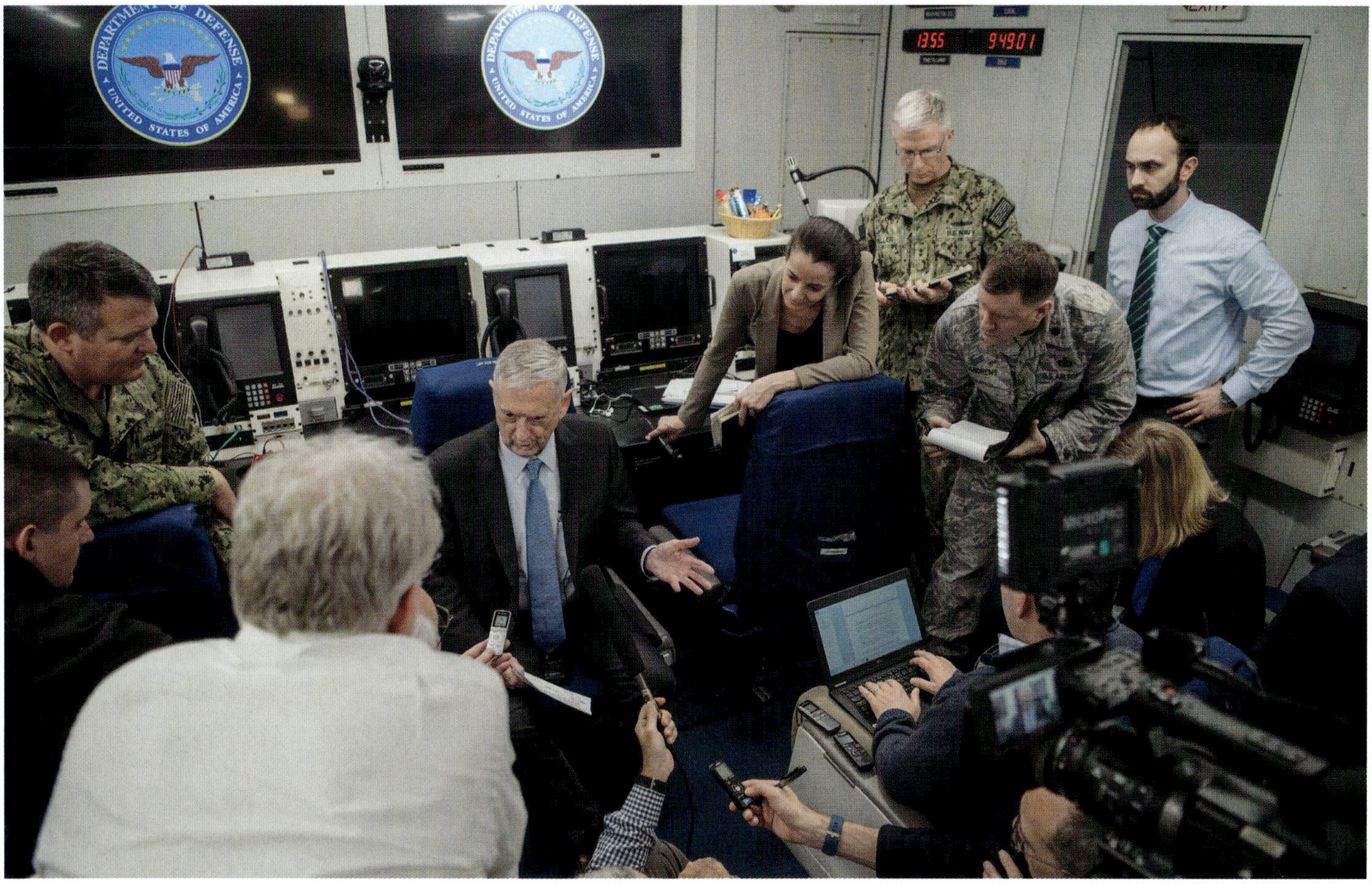

ABOVE: US Defence Secretary Jim Mattis holds a media briefing inside the Silver Bullet's communications compartment. USAF

trailer, which is easily recognised by the distinctive rounded shape and polished aluminium coachwork. This body shape dates back to the 1930s and is based on the Bowlus Road Chief, an earlier model of the all-aluminium travel trailer. This resulted in the trailer being nicknamed the 'Silver Bullet' by C-17 crews.

The Airstream was sectioned into three separate modules and further modified for easy transport aboard US military aircraft. The unit is bolted and strapped down on standard Air Force cargo pallets using standard Air Force Aerial Port loading systems.

Inside the 'Silver Bullet' is unique communications support and comfortable travel accommodation for high-ranking government officials. US Defence Secretaries have made the 'Silver Bullet' famous during their visits to war zones around the world. Donald Rumsfeld was particularly keen on using the aircraft to fly to airfields in Iraq and Afghanistan and made sure he was accompanied by a party of journalists, who filmed him meeting senior commanders and officials inside the 'Silver Bullet'.

Other senior leaders to use the 'Silver Bullet' included US Vice President Dick Chaney, and a select few military commanders who use the capability to stay in touch with the Pentagon and the White House during times of crisis. Other recent distinguished passengers included Drew Carey and Robin Williams, who used it to travel to entertain US troops in Iraq and Afghanistan.

RIGHT: US Vice President Dick Cheney was one of many senior US government leaders who made use of the Silver Bullet during visits to US troops in warzones around the Middle East. USAF

The 'Silver Bullet' provides its users with creature comforts, including their own bathroom, shower, galley, sitting and sleeping areas. It also has an integrated communications system capable of global reach, high-level, secure voice/data, and video teleconferencing. Specialised cables interface to the carrying aircraft's communications systems.

Originally, two 'Silver Bullet' were bought by the USAF and positioned at McGuire AFB in New Jersey, and Yokota Air Base in Japan. Responsibility for maintaining the capability has since passed to the 89th Airlift Wing at Joint Base Andrews in Maryland, which looks after Air Force One and other air transport for high-level government and military leaders.

For lower ranking officials or when the 'Silver Bullet' is not available, the USAF has procured a number of other VIP travel solutions that can be installed inside C-17s. It has bought several roll-on, roll-off palletised VIP seating systems from the US company, SelectTech. »

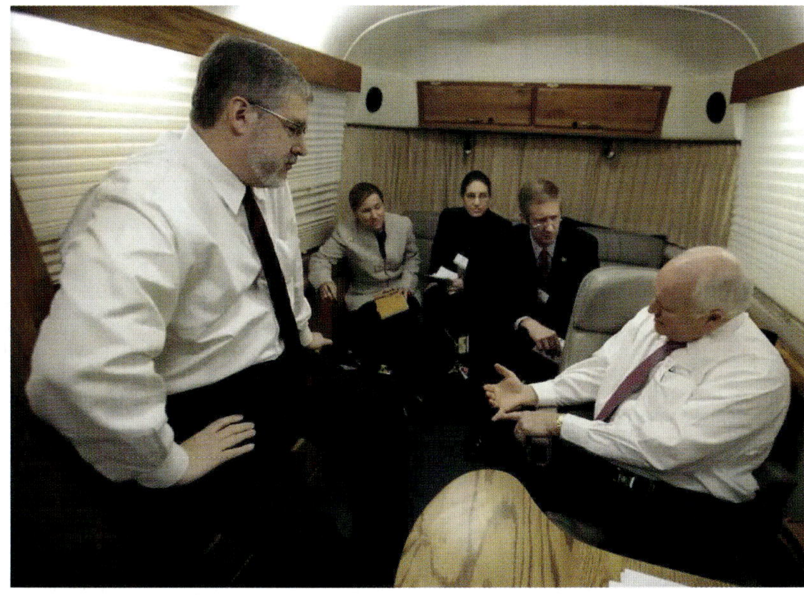

The Senior Leader In-transit Pallet, or SLIP, is an open seat-pallet, enabling dignitaries the ability to travel in cargo-type aircraft in relative comfort with power for computers, printers, and chargers, comfortable seats and a large worktable. Each four-chair SLIP can be connected to additional SLIPs using the same aircraft power connection. It is secured to the aircraft via the USAF Standard 463L Cargo System. The SLIP is currently certified for operations on C-17 and KC-10 and can be carried as cargo on Boeing KC-135R Stratotanker, Lockheed Martin C-130 Hercules, and C-5 aircraft.

An additional capability is SelectTech's SLICC, or Senior Leader In-transit Conference Capsule, which is a compartmentalised traveling suite designed specifically for dignitaries to work and rest while in transit. Its climate-controlled conference and sleeping modules can be used together or separately. The conference module provides work area for two people with connections for computers into a wall-mounted screen and can be connected to a Viper communications terminal, which provides in-transit secure and non-secure voice, data, and video

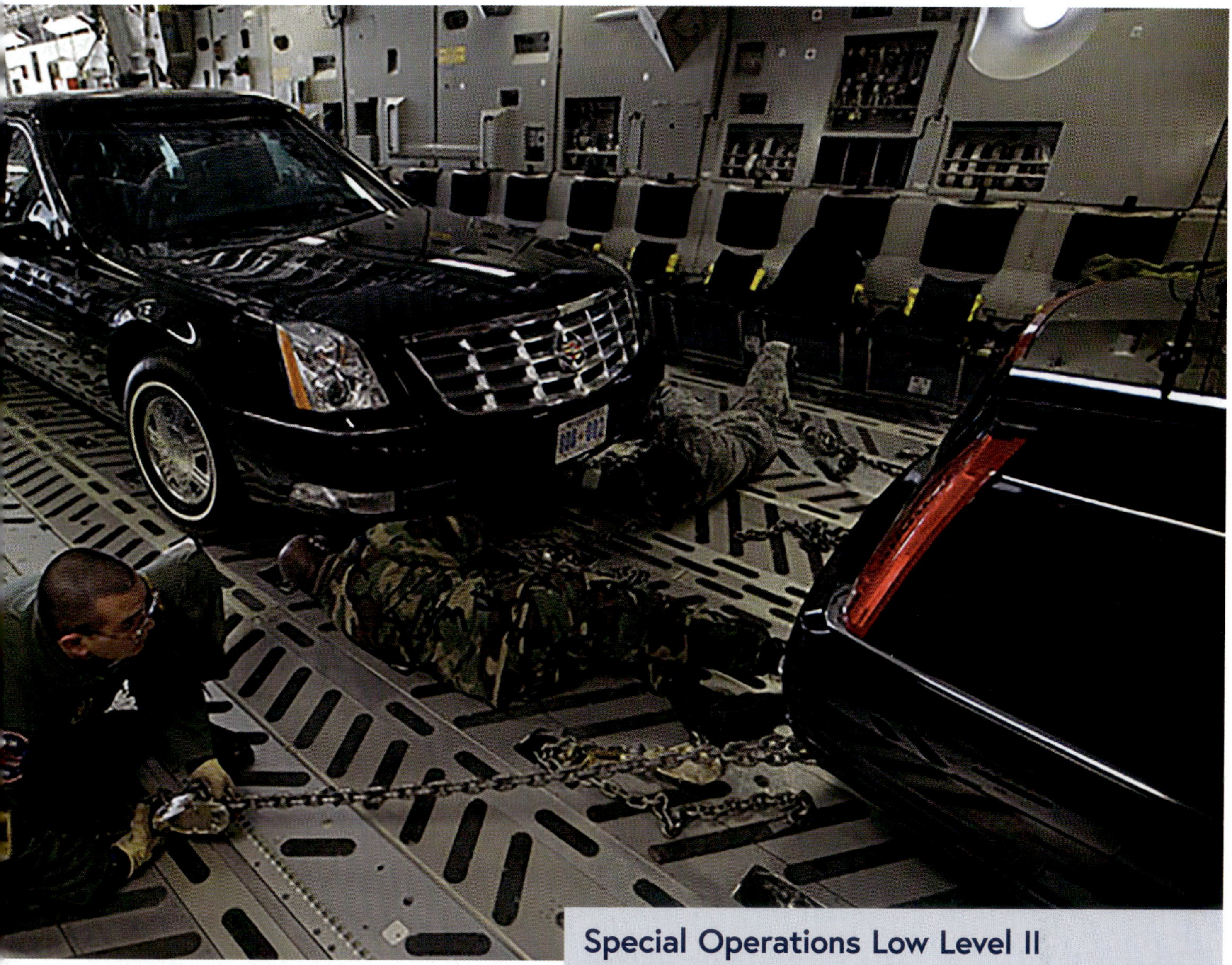

ABOVE: The US President's armoured limousine, known as 'The Beast', is routinely carried by C-17 ahead of visits by the American head of state to foreign countries. USAF

teleconferencing capability. The SLICC is certified on medium to large cargo aircraft including the C-17, C-130 and KC-10.

The USAF is in the process of replacing the 'Silver Bullet' with the Roll-on Conference Capsule (ROCC), which is also made by SelectTech. It includes intercom systems, lavatories, Ethernet network, Wi-Fi, video conferencing system display, external voice and data connectivity (wideband or narrowband), sleeping quarters and a nine-person conference room. The ROCC is intended to be used in the C-17 and C-130.

Special Operations Low Level II

The Special Operations Low Level II (SOLL II) mission was created in 1979 to fulfil requirements for a single vital mission, Desert One, the ill-fated mission to Iran to rescue US diplomats being held hostage in the Middle East country. Nine Lockheed C-141 Starlifter crews were trained in three basic tactics: night vision goggle (NVG) low level flight, NVG landing, and rapid offload.

In 1980, Military Airlift Command was directed to keep the capability indefinitely and C-141 crews at Charleston AFB in South Carolina took on the mission, which rapidly expanded during the 1980s to involve more than 20 special operations capabilities. Aircraft and crews were held at three hours' notice to move to fly highly classified missions for US Special Operations Command, the Joint Chiefs of Staff, and other government agencies.

The transition from the C-141 to C-17 saw the mission pass to the 437th Airlift Wing at Charleston AFB, with crews first seeing action in Afghanistan in 2001.

RIGHT: The Roll-on Conference Capsule (ROCC) is to replace the 'Silver Bullet'. SelectTech

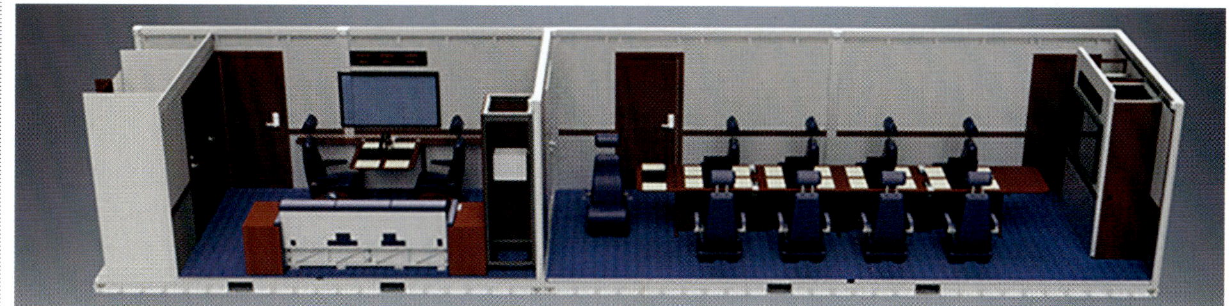

TO BOSNIA AND KOSOVO

C-17 Balkan Debut

As US Army troops started to approach the northern border of Bosnia in December 1995 to kick off NATO's peacekeeping mission in the war-torn country, the Sava River started to flood, blocking the American advance.

According to the official USAF history of the C-17, a pontoon bridge was needed, and fast. Transporting the sections via river barges from Germany would have been too slow, the rail system was unreliable, and US Army flatbed trailers could not haul the oversized sections through the German autobahn tollbooths.

The US Air Force had dispatched 18 of its then new McDonnell Douglas Boeing C-17A Globemaster IIIs, from the 436th Airlift Wing, to Rhein-Main Airbase in Germany to

LEFT: USAF C-17 crews at Rhein-Main Airbase had to keep their aircraft flying through the depth of the European winter. US DoD/Joint Combat Camera

BELOW: Rhein-Main Airbase, near Frankfurt in Germany, was the temporary home to the first overseas operational deployment of the C-17. US DoD/Joint Combat Camera

LEFT: Dozens of US Army Bradley combat vehicles were delivered to Tuzla airfield in Bosnia by C-17s to serve with NATO's Implementation Force (IFOR), which was mandated to police the Dayton Peace Accord.
US DoD/Joint Combat Camera

support the movement of 20,000 US troops to Bosnia. They were quickly ordered to airlift 25 pontoon bridge sections, each weighing 16 tons, to Taszar in Hungary.

They were soon put on trucks and driven to the banks of the Sava to allow the US Army engineers to complete the bridge, allowing the march south by the US armoured column to continue without delay.

This was the first of many 'mission firsts' for the C-17 which had earned a reputation in the USAF as 'a problem child' because of technical delays and cost overruns. As Operation Joint Endeavor unfolded, the C-17's unique and impressive capabilities were demonstrated time and time again.

For the first time, a C-17 transported a 40-foot side-loader for lifting containers off railroad cars, which were urgently needed to resupply US Army units. The Lockheed C-5 Galaxy had never moved the loader because of its unusual dimensions. With a taller and squarer cargo bay, the C-17 was able to take it into Taszar.

The C-17 outperformed the Lockheed C-141 Starlifter, which it was replacing across USAF Air Mobility Command, achieving a peak day of 1.8 million pounds of cargo moved into Bosnia and Hungary while the C-141's peak day was 565,000 pounds. According to Air Mobility Command statistics, the C-17 flew 26.6 percent of the intra theatre missions, 494 missions, moving 31.3 percent of the passengers, 2,965, and 55.9 percent of the cargo, 17,279 tons.

The C-17 was also the only aircraft capable of flying outsize cargo into the small airport of the Bosnian capital, Sarajevo. Its 8,530 feet long runway only had a useable length of 5,860 feet due to the existence of a tunnel that had »

BELOW: C-17 delivered sections of pontoon bridges to Hungary to help the US Army cross the Sava River.
US DoD/Joint Combat Camera

been dug under the runway by Bosnian troops. This meant C-141's cargo carrying capacity had to be reduced but a C-17 could land fully loaded.

French air force unloading teams at Sarajevo airport were also impressed by the ability of C-17 crews to unload 18 pallets in under 30 minutes, the same time it usually took a Lockheed C-130 Hercules crew to unload just four pallets.

Tuzla airfield also proved an ideal environment for the C-17. The airfield's taxi ways were too narrow for a C-5 to turn around on, so the giant airlifter could not be unloaded without closing airfield's main runway. A C-17 could turn easily on the airfield and unload cargoes in less than 23 minutes. They flew in a range of heavy vehicles, including self-propelled 155mm howitzers, Bradley fighting vehicles, snowploughs, and other large items.

"We made believers of a lot of folks who had not been necessarily in favour of the C-17. A lot of people suddenly realised the value of the airplane—its ability to get in and out of smaller runways with narrow taxiways and parking ramps, its turn ability, its roll-on roll-off loading capability, its large out-space cargo capability, plus its heavy lift ability makes it an ideal candidate for something like going into Bosnia," said USAF Major General Charles H. Coolidge Jr, NATO's director of the regional air movement coordination centre.

The C-17 drew high praise from US President Bill Clinton, who was especially impressed with the C-17's performance as he toured US bases in Europe, flying aboard the aircraft.

Just four years after the US military had intervened in Bosnia, its role in the Balkans expanded when fighting broke out in the Yugoslav province of Kosovo between ethnic Albanian insurgents and Serbian security forces. NATO launched an air campaign in a bid to force the Yugoslav military to withdraw from Kosovo. The US Army was ordered to deploy a task force of McDonnell Douglas AH-64A Apache attack helicopters to Albania to strike into Kosovo.

The 437th Airlift Wing dispatched 12 C-17s from Charleston AFB, along with 30 aircrews, to Ramstein Air Base, in April 1999 to begin moving Task Force Hawk from Germany

ABOVE: Rinas Airport, outside the Albanian capital Tirana, was the hub for the US airlift effort to deliver Task Force Hawk. Heavy rain turned the base into a quagmire for many weeks, adding to the difficulties faced by US personnel deploying to base.
US DoD/Joint Combat Camera

LEFT: The US C-17 fleet was tested to the full deploying Task Force Hawk to Albania, overcoming primitive airport facilities, limited ramp space and poor weather.
US DoD/Joint Combat Camera

to the Rinas Airport in Tirana, Albania. It comprised 24 AH-64 gunships, support helicopters, a multiple launch rocket system (MLRS) artillery battalion, a support battalion, a mechanised infantry company, a military police company, a signal company, military intelligence, aviation maintenance, and other support elements. Along with the Apaches, the C-17s airlifted 58 M2 Bradleys and 36 M1 Abram tanks.

Initially, flights into Tirana were restricted to daytime only operations due to the lack of radar and adequate instrument approach equipment. It took two weeks for the US Army to bring its own nighttime landing system to Tirana, to provide a 24-hour capability for the C-17s to land around the clock. By the end of April, the C-17s were flying 20 sorties a day to Albania from Germany, deploying Task Force Hawk and delivering humanitarian aid for refugees.

Operations into Rinas Airport further demonstrated the C-17's superior capability in operating into a small, poorly equipped airfield with outsize cargo loads.

For this constrained environment, the C-17 was especially well suited. C-17s discharged their load of pallets in less than 30 minutes. A single C-17 could fly four times the cargo and could fly further than a C-130, the other USAF airlifter flying into Rinas Airport. The C-17s and C-130s chalked up a combined launch reliability rate of 93 percent. Airfield conditions at Rinas, however, resulted in numerous tyre cuts and eight foreign object damage incidents.

In June, Task Force Falcon — drawn from the US Army's 1st Infantry Division — had to be rapidly redeployed to Skopje in Macedonia to join the NATO peacekeeping force that was soon to enter Kosovo. Twelve C-17s flew 16-hour missions with extra pilots and loadmasters augmenting the crew to pull off the deployment. The aircraft lifted 70-ton M1A1 tanks and Bradley fighting vehicles into Skopje

as well as moving 2,525 personnel and 11,886 tons of cargo.

According to the USAF official history of the C-17, during the Kosovo crisis, C-17s flew 799 of the 1,108 strategic airlift mission, which compared to 205 and 104 missions, respectively, by C-5s and the C141s, with the commercial carriers performing another 66 missions. During the Task Force Hawk deployment, C-17s flew 468 intra-theatre missions while the C-130s flew up 269 missions. During the Task Force Falcon deployment, C-17s also flew 253 missions.

Neither Task Force Hawk or Falcon fired a shot in anger during the Kosovo crisis, but the USAF's airlift support was essential to their deployments and further demonstrated that the C-17 was now a very mature aircraft, which was delivering for the American taxpayer.

ABOVE: Rinas Airport was a hive of activity from April 1999, as the US Air Force and US Army turned it into a full up forward operating base for AH-64 Apache attack helicopters. US DoD/Joint Combat Camera

BELOW: The 437th Airlift Wing from Charleston AFB provided the core of the C-17 fleet for the Albanian operation. US DoD/ Joint Combat Camera

INTO AFGHANISTAN
2001

USAF C-17 Operations in Afghanistan

On November 25, 2001, 300 US Marines aboard six helicopters undertook a nighttime assault on an airstrip in southern Afghanistan, securing the area and naming it Forward Operating Base (FOB) Rhino. Three days later under the cover of darkness and using night vision goggles (NVGs), the first Boeing C-17 Globemaster IIIs set down on the hard-packed desert soil, offloading more personnel and cargo. Between November 28, 2001, and January 4, 2002, C-17 Special Operations Low Level II (SOLL II) qualified crews of the 437th Airlift Wing flew 64 sorties onto the airstrip, aiding in the effort to establish the forward base as America's first military base in Afghanistan.

The most important aspect of the environment at FOB Rhino was the fact that it was the definition of a small austere airfield. It was a semi-prepared surface, meaning it was not paved but hard-packed sand, grated and marked with large rocks on the perimeter. In simple terms it was a "dirt" strip determined to be suitable for landing a large aircraft on.

The first wave of C-17s that landed were transporting Seabees construction engineers and their heavy plant, which was used to maintain the landing surface so more reinforcements could be flown in. Over the next eight days, the C-17s delivered 1,450 tons of cargo, and 481 passengers to help the US Marines build up their base.

This operation also marked the first use of NVGs during combat by C-17A SOLL II crews. As a result of this success, NVG training became the norm for all C-17 crews, not just specialised tactical crews.

The opening up of FOB Rhino to C-17 operations was also a major milestone for the USAF C-17 force,

LEFT: Karshi-Khanabad, or K-2, air base in southeastern Uzbekistan, was the airlift hub for USAF C-17s supporting US Special Operations Forces moving into Northern Afghanistan in response to the 9/11 attacks. US DoD/Joint Combat Camera

BELOW: A stream of USAF airlifters, including C-17s, started to flow into Afghanistan after US Marines captured airfields in the south of the central Asian country. US DoD/Joint Combat Camera

ABOVE: C-17s assigned to the 817th Expeditionary Airlift Squadron operated from Rhein-Main Airbase in Germany and then from Incirlik Airbase in Turkey to support airlift missions across the Middle East and Afghanistan. One of its C-17s visited Manas in Kyrgyzstan in 2014 en route to Afghanistan. US DoD/Joint Combat Camera

which would spend the next 20 years flying in and out of Afghanistan. This was the original 'forever war'.

In just over a year's time, US President George W Bush would dispatch American troops to invade Iraq to open a new front in what was now known as the 'Global War on Terrorism'. Soon the US military was operating across the Middle East, Africa and even in the Philippines to hunt down acolytes of the 9/11 mastermind, Osama bin Laden. Wherever US troops went, they were invariable flown to these combat zones on C-17s.

Over 20 years, active duty, reserve and Air National Guard C-17 crews criss-crossed the world carrying cargo and people. Ramstein, Sigonella, Rota, Souda Bay, Guam, Mildenhall, Diego Garcia, Al Udeid, Al Dahfra, Ali Al Salem, Al Assad, Erbil, Baghdad, Tripoli, Amman, Thumrait, Djibouti, Kandahar, Bagram, Kabul, K-2 and Manas, were just some of the stop off points of C-17 crews.

Over this period, USAF C-17-squadron commanders rarely ever had all their aircraft and personnel at the same location. Being deployed became the norm for C-17 crews.

RIGHT: Bringing home America's fallen soldiers. A US Army honour guard carry the casket of a fallen soldier from a C-17 during ramp ceremony at Dover AFB in July 2009. US DoD/Joint Combat Camera

PARACHUTE DROP

C-17s Delivers the 173rd Airborne Brigade

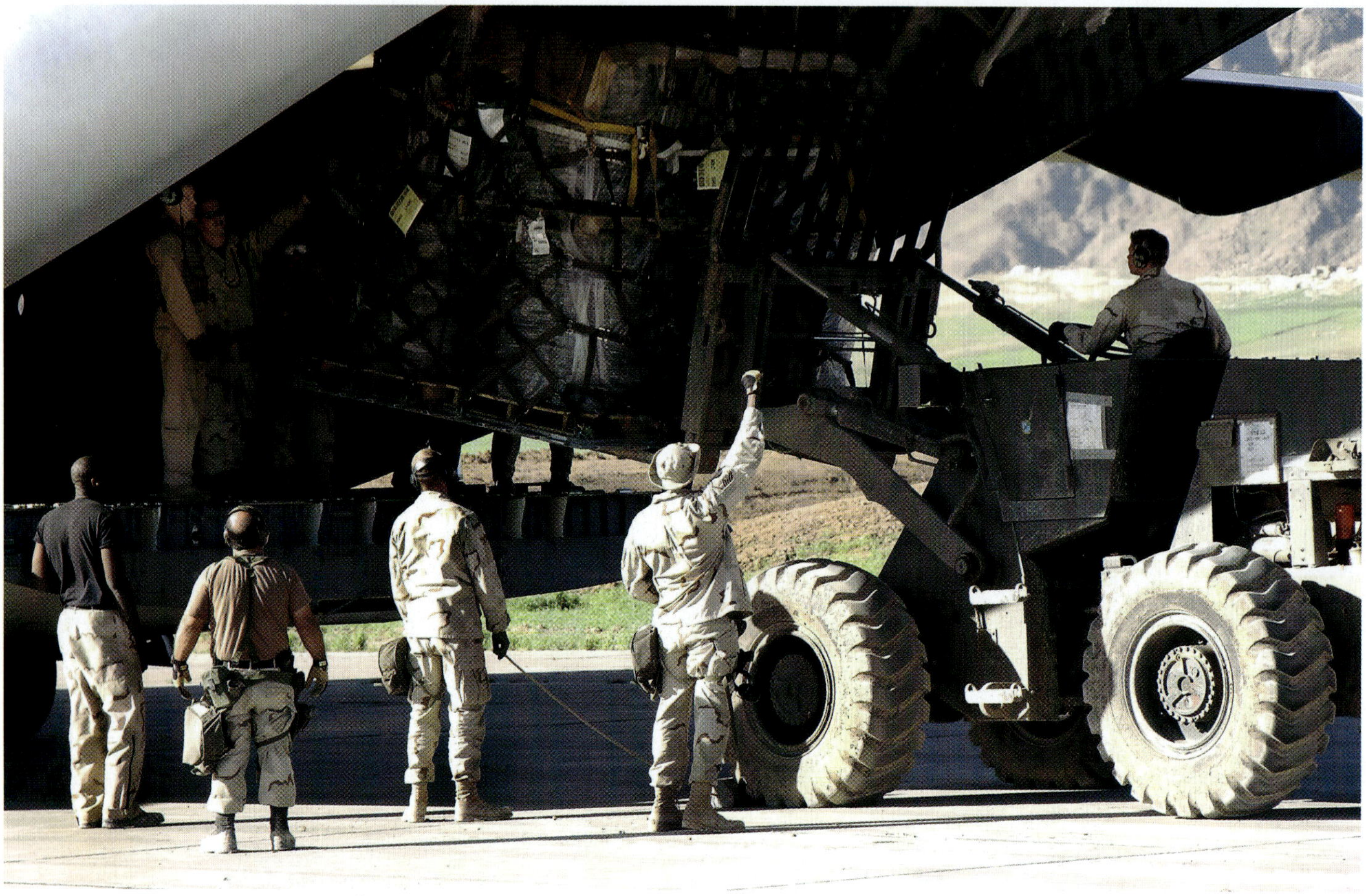

ABOVE: A shuttle of C-17s kept the 173rd Airborne Brigade at Bashur airfield resupplied as it opened a northern front against Saddam Hussein' army. US DoD/Joint Combat Camera

Operation Northern Delay was intended to deliver a brigade of US paratroopers into Iraq to open a new front against Saddam Hussein's army. It was hoped the move would distract Iraqi troops from the main advance by US tank columns on Baghdad from Kuwait.

The drop was set for the night of March 26, 2003, and would be first combat jump by US paratroopers since the 1989 invasion of Panama. Spearheading the operation was the Italy-based 173rd Airborne Brigade and it launched from Aviano Airbase in northern Italy onboard 17 Boeing C-17 Globemaster IIIs of the 62nd, 446th, 437th and 315th Airlift Wings.

After Turkey closed its airspace to US forces, the formation of C-17s had to make the long journey over the Eastern Mediterranean, Jordan and western Iraq to reach the drop zone on Bashur Airfield in the Kurdish region of northern Iraq.

In the first wave, 954 paratroopers jumped on the drop zone, exiting the aircraft in under 58 seconds. The force

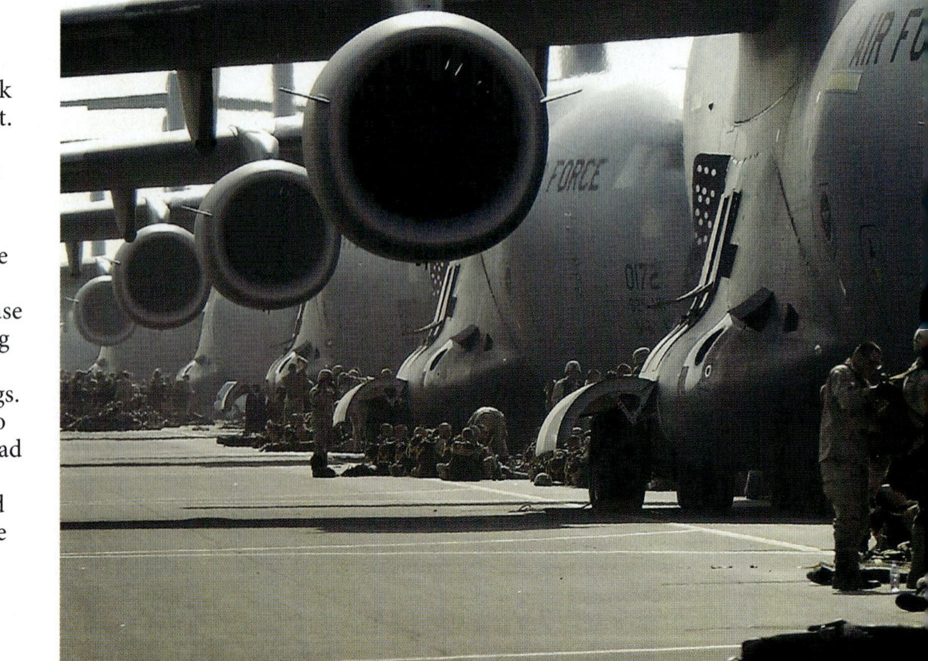

RIGHT: Paratroopers of the 173rd Airborne Brigade prep for action at Aviano Airbase in Italy as they countdown for the launch of Operation Northern Delay. US DoD/Joint Combat Camera

had been strung out over a 10,000-metre drop zone, and it took 15 hours before it was completely assembled. Once on the ground the US paratroopers linked up with anti-Saddam Kurdish Peshmerga fighters who controlled the region.

Over the next five nights, more C-17s flown by pilots using night vision goggles, delivered the full brigade of 2,000 soldiers, several M1A1 Abrams tanks, 400 vehicles, and 3,000 tons of equipment into the austere, unimproved airfield, opening up the northern front against Saddam Hussein's army.

This was not the last tactical airlift operation flown by the C-17 during Operation Iraqi Freedom. Out in the desert region of Western Iraq, elite US Special Operations Forces (SOF) were launching a hit and run campaign to neutralise Iraqi Scud missile batteries threatening Israel.

Special Operations Low Level II (SOLL-II) C-17 crews from Charleston AFB in South Carolina, qualified in nighttime tactical missions, grouped into the 781st Expeditionary Airlift Squadron (EAS), flew several missions to set up improvised forward arming and refuelling points (SOF) on roads in remote area to allow US SOF helicopters to refuel. These then became temporary staging bases for raiding missions.

US SOF commander then decided to capture the Iraqi airbase at H-1 to turn it into forward operating. After SOF raiders seized the air base, SOLL II crews flew 10 M1A1 Abrams tanks into the base to boost US firepower.

As the Iraqi regime was teetering after US ground forces pushed into Baghdad, the SOLL II C-17 crews were tasked with moving the Combined Forces Land Component Commander's Early Entry Command Post vehicles to Baghdad International Airport (BIAP). This enabled senior US Army commanders to oversee the final defeat of the Iraqi army and occupation of the country's capital.

In the official US Air Force history of the C-17 programme, the aircraft operations were dubbed a major success, adding, "unequivocally, the C-17 has proven itself in the combat environment, leaving its acquisition troubles behind."

ABOVE: C-17s operated across the Middle East during Operation Iraqi Freedom to supply US forces across the region, as well as enabling the deployment of US Army combat units. US DoD/Joint Combat Camera

LEFT: Seventeen C-17s were massed at Aviano Airbase in Italy to launch the opening combat parachute of Operation Northern Delay. US DoD/Joint Combat Camera

BUILDING THE AFGHAN AIRBRIDGE – EVERY DAY

RAF C-17s Operations to Afghanistan 2006-2014

A sign at the entrance to RAF Brize Norton in 2010 proudly declared the Oxfordshire air base was to be the UK's 'gateway to operations'. The array of nearly 20 large military and civilian transport aircraft parked on its huge Cold War era ramp area confirmed that it had become the crucial hub in the UK logistic campaign in Afghanistan.

Everyday military and civilian aircraft loaded with passengers and cargo departed from RAF Brize Norton for Afghanistan to sustain what was dubbed the 'air bridge'. More than 90% of the UK's strategic airlift capability was committed to sustaining the Afghan air bridge during Operation Herrick, as the British campaign in the central Asian country was codenamed.

At the heart of building the air bridge in 2010, was Wing Commander Steve Foster-Bazin, and his small Operations Wing team.

LEFT: 99 Squadron kept open the RAF's 'air bridge' to Afghanistan throughout Operation Herrick, moving troops and cargo to the central Asian country.
MOD/Crown Copyright

BELOW: RAF C-17s flew almost everything the British Army needed to fight its war in Afghanistan, including Royal Navy Sea King radar surveillance helicopters.
MOD/Crown Copyright

"I co-ordinate activity in terms of airfield output and the management of our aircraft away from base" he said in 2010. "We manage the flying programme. The Defence Supply Chain Operations and Movements (DSCOM) arbitrate what goes by air, sea or land. There is a regular planning meeting every several months to determine the plan for

When British Army vehicles started to be attacked by roadside improvised bombs, 99 Squadron was tasked to fly up-armoured vehicles, including Warriors to Afghanistan. MOD/Crown Copyright

moving things by air. The detailed plan is given to us a few days before aircraft have to fly. We firefight this when things change, in co-ordination with DSCOM and manage the impact on future operations."

"Some charter fights service use airfields nearer to troop garrisons around the UK and Germany but the vast majority of UK passengers and cargo to Afghanistan delivered by air comes through here," said Foster-Bazin. "We have a 24-hour cell here that oversees the movement of our aircraft. The aircraft plot is managed continuously. Charter flights are managed directly by DSCOM at Abbey Wood in Bristol."

During an average week just under a thousand people left RAF Brize Norton for Afghanistan but this could surge during the rotation or relief in place (RIP) every six months that the British task force is in the central Asian country. "Over a RIP – an eight-to-nine-week period – we move 22,000 people in and out of Afghanistan" said Foster-Bazin.

Since 2001, the backbone of the RAF's air cargo movement operation had been its fleet of Boeing C-17A Globemaster III strategic transport aircraft. Four aircraft were initially leased but subsequently it was decided to buy them outright. Two additional aircraft had been added by 2010, and a seventh aircraft joined the RAF Brize Norton-based 99 Squadron by the end of that year.

"The C-17 is not an air asset – it's a logistic campaign asset," Wing Commander Simon Edwards, 99 Squadron's officer commanding in 2010 said at the time.

BELOW:
Kandahar Airfield in southern Afghanistan was the main hub for RAF C-17 operations until the airfield at Camp Bastion in Helmand was upgraded to take the giant airlifters.
Tim Ripley

Camp Bastion airfield was built from scratch in the centre of the Helmand desert. In the final years of the British presence in Helmand province, C-17 flew directly into the base. MOD/Crown Copyright

He reported that 90% of the squadron's missions then were flown in support of Operation Herrick. "Four of our aircraft are operational on any given day" he said. "We are really getting the most out of the aircraft".

99 Squadron launched a C-17 out of RAF Brize Norton every day, bound for Afghanistan and it carried all the UK helicopters, armoured fighting vehicles (including Danish Leopard tanks) and ammunition required to sustain UK-led Task Force Helmand. According to Edwards, it was almost impossible to use charter aircraft to carry ammunition to Afghanistan. "The UK could not wage the Afghan campaign the way it does without the C-17," he said. "If the UK military needs to move big things quickly, we do it."

Edwards described the C-17 as an "incredibly reliable" aircraft and said it had an "unshakeable reputation" in the UK armed forces.

As well as its cargo carrying role, 99 Squadron was responsible for recovering the bulk of the UK military casualties from Afghanistan.

"We maintain perpetual readiness to collect wounded soldiers when the need is most," said Edwards. "We fly them directly from the main British base at Camp Bastion in Helmand Province to Birmingham International Airport to deliver casualties to Selly Oak hospital. Crews have a 24-hour working day on these missions. We are doing more aero medical evacuations (aeromed) than ever before. We can fly six missions in six days, or in six months."

The crews of 99 Squadron also had the solemn duty for flying home the bodies of fallen British soldiers from Afghanistan.

"After an initial honeymoon in the weeks after the first jet was delivered in May 2001, we never came home from Exercise Saif Sareea II in Oman in the autumn of that year," he said. "We have been going full throttle since 2002. There has been no obvious change in tempo. We did not notice when we withdrew from Iraq in 2009. We did not get a day off. I have never had squadron in the one place on one day. Only twice have I had all my aircraft at RAF Brize Norton."

In 2010, 99 squadron had 334 personnel, including some 100 aircrew, around 200 engineers and 24 support staff.

The serviceability of the C-17 fleet was enhanced by an upgrade programme in the United States to bring the first four RAF aircraft up to the same configuration as the second batch of aircraft to be delivered. Although this resulted in a temporary restriction on non-Afghan C-17 operations in the longer term it resulted in greater fleet availability and reliability, according to Edwards.

A major element in the RAF airbridge operation was the use of what were termed 'slip air crews' at

BELOW: RAF Brize Norton in Oxfordshire is the home of 99 Squadron and it served as the home hub of C-17 operations throughout the Afghan campaign. Tim Ripley

forward airbases across the Middle East at Minhad in the United Arab Emirates (UAE), Al Udeid in Qatar and RAF Akrotiri on Cyprus.

The slip crews allowed the tempo of operations to be maintained at a high level and ensure aircraft are not on the ground waiting for crews to rest between missions. Forward bases were also needed because the hot-high conditions in Afghanistan limit the fuel load and range of aircraft operating there.

The footprint for the forward deployed air crews was constantly changed as the focus of British logistic operations evolved. When the UAE became the focus of the delivery of protected mobility vehicles by sea and air into Afghanistan in 2009, 99 Squadron began forward deploying a C-17 with maintenance support and an aircrew to Minhad. The vehicles were delivered by ship to the UAE and then the C-17s shuttled them into Camp Bastion. According to Edwards, a daily flight took place from the UAE into Camp Bastion.

A slip crew was also positioned at Al Udeid to take over from the crew of any aircraft outbound from the UK to fly on the last leg into Afghanistan. He said at any one time two C-17 crews would be based as slip crews in the Middle East. "They make the airbridge work," he said. "The UAE-based aircraft was also very useful to use when we had to start flying humanitarian aid to Pakistan after the earthquake that hit the country."

In 2010, there seemed little prospect that the Afghan war would end anytime soon. The C-17 crews steeled themselves to keep the air bridge open indefinitely.

Wing Commander Edwards commented at the time, "We are fully resourced, we busy but fully manned and have enough people for the job at hand without burning people out. We are coping, so we can go on for many years."

The C-17 crews of 99 Squadron had to continue flying Operation Herrick missions to Afghanistan for four more years when Britain's combat mission in the country concluded. This would not be the end of the road for 99 Squadron's involvement in Afghanistan.

BOTTOM: 99 Squadron had the solemn duty of returning fallen British soldiers from Afghanistan to RAF Lyneham and then RAF Brize Norton. MOD/Crown Copyright

ABOVE: In June 2021, 99 flew the last British garrison from Kabul's Hamid Karzai International Airport to bring Operation Toral to a close, ending 20 years of a permanent UK presence in the central Asian country. Less than two months later, 99 Squadron returned to Kabul to evacuate civilians from the city. MOD/Crown Copyright

THE MOOSE'S FINEST HOUR

C-17s in Kabul Evacuation

Day after day, dozens of giant US Air Force Boeing C-17A Globemaster IIIs touched down at Kabul's beleaguered civil airport to lift thousands of refugees to safety. In just 17 days of monumental effort, more than 100 USAF C-17s had flown just under 80,000 people out of Afghanistan.

It is not an exaggeration to say that without the huge capacity of the C-17s, Operation Allies Refuge would not have happened. When images emerged of more than 800 Afghans sitting on the floor of a C-17's cargo hold, they made the front pages of newspapers around the world.

That was not the only iconic image of a C-17 during the evacuation. At the same time as aircraft callsign Reach 871 was breaking the C-17s load carrying record, harrowing scenes of desperate Afghans overrunning the airport's sole runway and hanging onto the side of a USAF C-17 were going viral on social media.

Amid this chaos and mayhem, the USAF's C-17 crews kept their aircraft flying into a Kabul's Hamid Karzai International Airport and in less than two weeks they had pulled off a miracle.

By mid-July 2021, US forces had largely withdrawn from Afghanistan except for a few hundred troops guarding the US Embassy in the centre of Kabul. Others protected a few terminal buildings at the airport on the northern edge of the city. Across the country Taliban forces were relentlessly advancing. It was only a matter of time before they were at the gates of Kabul.

The USAF's Air Mobility Command was already preparing to mobilise a huge armada of aircraft to lift out the last Americans from Kabul. Aircraft were on standby

in the Middle East and C-17s were already shuttling into Kabul with extra US troops, a contingent of Sikorsky HH-60H Rescue Hawk helicopters, and a new command team, led by a former US Navy SEAL, Rear Admiral Peter Vasely.

Airbases across the Middle East started to receive a first wave of additional C-17s to ready for the evacuation. Al Udeid Airbase in Qatar was the main US airlift hub in the Middle East and was already the home to the 816th Expeditionary Airlift Squadron of C-17s on temporary duty to the region. Additional ramp space for C-17s was found at Ali Al Salem Airbase in Kuwait and Al Dhafra Air Base in the United Arab Emirates.

Fast forward to August 11, Admiral Vasely and his command team in Kabul reported up to the head of US forces in the Middle East, General Ken McKenzie, that there was a growing threat to Kabul and enhanced security was needed to keep the airport open to allow the evacuation of remaining embassy staff, US passport holders, and other civilians with permission to leave by the President Joe Biden's August 31 deadline. Vasely feared that the Afghan army would melt away, leaving US and allied personnel at the mercy of the Taliban.

The following morning, President Biden signed off the plan, which involved three more battalions of troops being sent to Kabul airport to establish a security ring.

The first battalion of US Marines started arriving on C-17s from its forward base in Kuwait on Friday August 13. It was planned that the first of several thousand civilians who had worked with US forces, including Afghan interpreters and their families, would start flying out early the following week. »

LEFT: Chaos engulfed Hamid Karzai International Airport on the morning of August 16 as thousands of desperate Afghans tried to flee the country by climbing onboard any aircraft they could find. Several died after climbing on the side of a USAF C-17 just as it was moving to take off. The video footage was instantly shared around the world on social media. Social media, via You Tube

LEFT: In the early hours of August 15, the US Embassy in downtown Kabul was evacuated, with a helicopter shuttle moving hundreds of Americans to the city international airport. US DoD/ Joint Combat Camera

US reinforcements was still underway and several C-17s that on been on approach to the airport, including one carrying the USAF colonel who was due to take charge of running the evacuation operation, were forced to circle overhead before returning to Al Udeid. The colonel reported that the airport looked like a crowded football stadium during a riot, with thousands upon thousands of people outside trying to cram through the various gates and thousands more running onto the tarmac and taxiways like they were a pitch.

US Marine Corps air traffic controllers took over the airport tower in a bid to restore flight operations. US Army, Turkish and British troops were sent over to try to clear the runway.

As this mayhem was unfolding, a C-17 of the 6th Airlift Squadron was on the ground at the airport. The aircraft's captain ordered his crew to finish up loading and get as many people onboard as possible, so he could get airborne. Normal loading procedures were put aside and the loadmaster was not able to create a passenger manifest until they were off the ground. By the time aircraft, callsign Reach 871, was airborne it was clear that they were way over the previous record for the number of passengers carried by a C-17, 670 people. When they landed at Al Udeid, the passenger count had reached 823. This was more than double the routine peacetime passenger load.

When dawn broke on August 16 the Afghan civilians were still inside

ABOVE: USAF C-17 callsign Reach 871 broke aviation records when it took off from Kabul on August 15 carrying 823 people. US DoD/Joint Combat Camera

RIGHT: The mayhem that enveloped Kabul airport's main runway could be seen from space, with satellite imagery showing thousands of civilians being kept at bay by a thin line of allied troops. This kept the refugees away from the loading ramps, where several US and allied aircraft were stuck on the ground. Google Earth

The Afghans feared they would be persecuted if the Taliban took power.

This all changed during the evening of August 13, when the US Ambassador in Kabul and Admiral Vasely learned that Taliban fighters were on the outskirts of the city. They ordered the evacuation of the US Embassy to a temporary location in the State Department's aviation complex at the airport. This set in motion the helicopter airlift the Green Zone compound in downtown Kabul that was filmed live by the international news media. The Afghan president and several of his ministers then headed to the airport and commandeered an Afghan air force aircraft to fly out of the county.

Hours after the Afghan leaders had made their escape, tens of thousands of desperate Afghans began swarming into the civilian side of the airport to try to get on any aircraft they could. Once inside the airport, they soon made their way on to the main runway preventing any aircraft taking off or landing. The in-flow of

the airport. Crowds were swarming towards C-17s trying to get onboard. When one aircraft, serial 02-1109, tried to taxi to the runway to take off, hundreds of Afghans ran alongside, several climbed inside the undercarriage bays, hoping to hitch a ride to safety. When the aircraft finally got airborne, harrowing video footage showed Afghans falling to their deaths. Human remains were also found inside the aircraft's wheel well when it landed at Al Udeid. An inquiry by senior USAF officers and legal investigators subsequently cleared the aircraft crew of any wrongdoing, with a USAF spokesperson, saying, they "faced an unprecedented and rapidly-deteriorating security situation, and the crew's "airmanship and quick thinking ensured the safety of the crew and their aircraft."

It took several hours to clear the civilians out and reopen the runway. More ominously armed Taliban fighters had set up checkpoints around the perimeter. A new plan was now required. Admiral Vasely was ordered to reach out to the Taliban to find out if they would let the US and its allies continue to evacuate their people through the airport. Much to everyone's surprise, the Taliban said they would give their Americans until the end of the month to complete their evacuation.

It was now down to Air Mobility Command to mobilise dozens more C-17s to begin airlifting several »

thousand people a day out of the Kabul. The call went out to every C-17 base across the US and soon more than 100 jets – half the USAF, Air Force Reserve and Air National Guard's fleet – were heading to the Middle East to ramp up the operation. A formation of C-17s flew direct from the US, using air-to-air refuelling, to deliver three battalions of paratroopers from the 82nd Airborne Division to Kabul without landing at a staging airport. These aircraft then staged back to US airbases in Kuwait, Qatar and the UAE to begin shuttling into Kabul to pick up evacuees. Air Mobility Command then began mobilising a stream of other USAF and chartered aircraft to move the refugees from the airbases in the Gulf to other downstream locations which had better infrastructure to house and feed them. Choreographing all the moving parts of Operation Allies Refuge stretched Air Mobility Command to the limit.

Each day an air tasking order was issued to the participating air forces, allocating them landing slots at Kabul. To reduce the time the USAF C-17s needed to spend on the ground, Boeing KC-135 Stratotankers and McDonnell Douglas KC-10 Extenders, were on hand in orbits near Kabul to refuel the airlifters after they had left the Afghan capital.

During the last week of August, the airlift moved into high gear with dozens of USAF C-17 sorties each day lifting thousands of people to safety. The aircraft were routinely carrying

400 or 500 people at time. Several babies were born on board the aircraft, leading to one being named Reach, after the callsign of the USAF C-17 aircraft.

As the airlift was drawing to a close, tension started to rise around the airport as rogue terrorist groups threatened to attack US and allied forces. A suicide bomber struck near one of the gates to the airport on August 26, killing 13 US servicemen and hundreds of civilians. Several US personnel were seriously injured.

A C-17 of the 21st Airlift Squadron was mobilised from Al Udeid to fly to Kabul to pick up the casualties who were in need of life-saving medical treatment. The power generators at Kabul airport had

ABOVE: Peacetime loading limits were routinely dropped by USAF C-17 captains to get as many evacuees as possible onto their aircraft. US DoD/ Joint Combat Camera

LEFT: Every day more than a dozen USAF C-17s took off from Kabul airport, while US Marines and 82nd Airborne troopers secured its perimeter. US DoD/ Joint Combat Camera

C-17s loaded with evacuees took off from Kabul and headed for US-controlled airbases in the Arabian Gulf region, where they were moved onto waiting aircraft to take them to refugee camps around the world. US DoD/Joint Combat Camera

been put out of action in a sabotage attack so the C-17 had to land in darkness. The aircraft had to wait two hours on the tarmac with the aircraft's engines running because some of the critically wounded passengers were just out of surgery and needed to be stabilized before transport.

To reach Ramstein Airbase in Germany a KC-135 tanker on 'strip alert' in the Middle East had to be scrambled to refuel the C-17. The aircraft conducted a tricky mid-air refuelling at night over the Black Sea, while in its cargo bay a critical care team performed emergency surgery on a wounded patient. »

RIGHT: A loadmaster organises a column of evacuees as they prepare to board a USAF C-17. Most of the evacuees did not speak English and had never flown before, making securing the passengers difficult and time consuming. US DoD/ Joint Combat Camera

Operation Allies Refuge was scheduled to wrap up on August 30 and detailed preparations were made to recover the last US soldiers from Kabul airport under the cover of darkness. Even in the last 24 hours of operations, C-17 crews managed to rescue 1,250 additional evacuees.

In the hours before the deadline, under the cover of darkness a formation of five C-17s landed to extract the last 800 soldiers of the 82nd Airborne Division, the US ambassador and the US senior command team. Major General Chris Donahue, commander of the 82nd Airborne, was filmed on a night vision camera walking up the ramp of the final C-17 to leave the airport, marking the end of the evacuation.

The C-17 fleet's work was not over. Many of the refugees still had to be moved out of the Gulf airbases and all the personnel and equipment that had supported the operation had to be returned to home bases. One of the final missions was flown to the Pakistani capital Islamabad to recover three HH-60H, which had flown over Taliban held territory from Kabul in the final hours of the evacuation.

Operation Allies Refuge has been dubbed the largest humanitarian airlift since the 1948 Berlin airlift, which saw to the successful evacuation of 124,334 individuals. During the

RIGHT: After 13 US Marines were killed in a suicide bombing while guarding the airport perimeter, their bodies were returned home on a C-17, callsign Reach 824, of the New York Air National Guard. US DoD/Joint Combat Camera

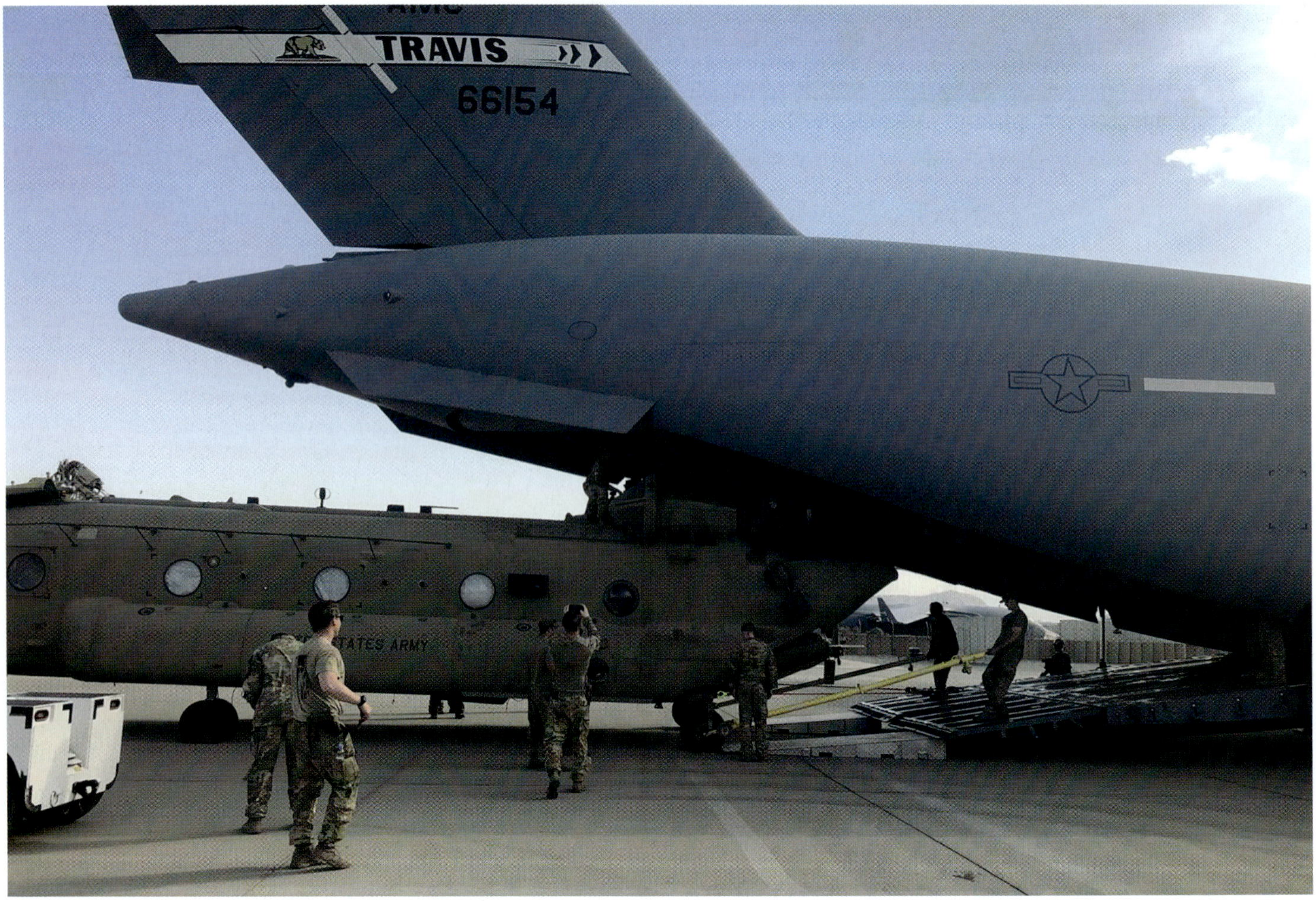

BELOW: As the airlift of civilians from Kabul wound down, attention turned to recovering important military equipment to prevent it falling into the hands of Taliban. US Army CH-47 Chinook helicopters were lifted out of Kabul on USAF C-17s. US DoD/Joint Combat Camera

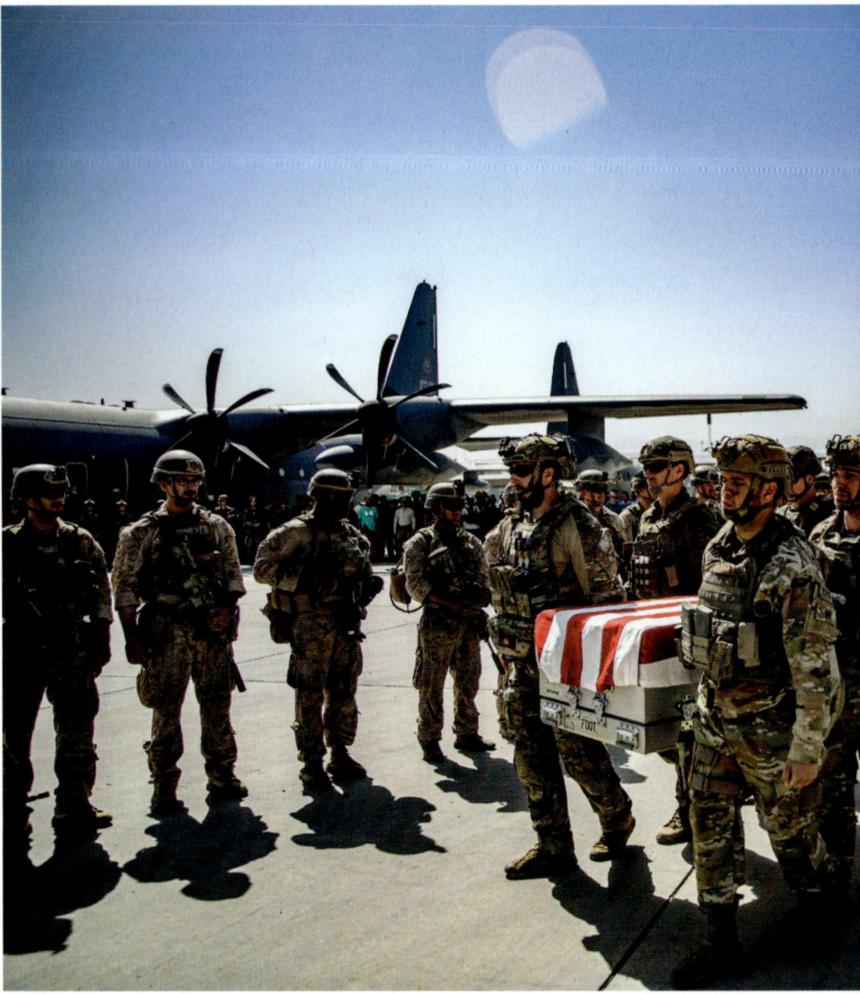

17 days of evacuation efforts, more than 500 USAF active duty, reserve and National Guard aircrews flew missions around the clock. Some 330 USAF C-17 missions were flown in and out of Hamid Karzai International Airport, evacuating more than 79,000 people, including 6,000 Americans. They also withdrew more than 5,500 military personnel and their equipment. On average, 7,500 civilians were evacuated daily, with the high point being August 23, when more than 21,600 civilians were evacuated every 34 minutes.

ABOVE: Major General Chris Donahue was the last US soldier to leave Kabul in the early hours of August 30, stepping onto the tail ramp of a USAF C-17. US DoD/ Joint Combat Camera

LEFT: A formation of five USAF C-17s lifted out the last rear-guard of 82nd Airborne Division troopers from Kabul in the August 30. US DoD/ Joint Combat Camera

ABOVE: Thousands of desperate Afghans waited for days in the hot summer sun to board RAF C-17s to fly them out of Kabul to safety. MOD/Crown Copyright

RAF C-17s IN OPERATION PITTING

Britain's Kabul Evacuation

"It was almost irreplaceable", was how one senior Royal Air Force officer described the role of 99 Squadron's Boeing C-17A Globemaster III in the evacuation from Kabul in August 2021. "On some occasions, size is the most important attribute. The C-17 showed unquestionable utility – it underwrote the success of the operation."

In Britain's Permanent Joint Headquarters at Northwood, on the outskirts of London, intelligence officers and planning staff were watching events with some alarm as the Taliban were relentlessly advancing on Kabul and drawing up contingency plans. The main RAF airlift hubs in the Gulf, at Minhad Air Base in the United Arab Emirates and RAF Akrotiri on Cyprus, were put on alert to be ready to launch aircraft should an emergency non-combatant evacuation (NEO) be ordered.

At the end of July, 99 Squadron at its RAF Brize Norton home was warned off to be ready to play its part in the mission, which was already dubbed Operation Pitting. On August 6, the squadron was

RIGHT: To kick-start Britain's evacuation operation, hundreds of Paratroopers from 16 Air Assault Brigade were flown to Kabul on RAF C-17s to help secure the city's airport. MOD/Crown Copyright

alerted to have two C-17s and five crews at five days' notice to move. Events started to move fast the following week, with the first C-17 departing from RAF Brize Norton for Minhad on August 11.

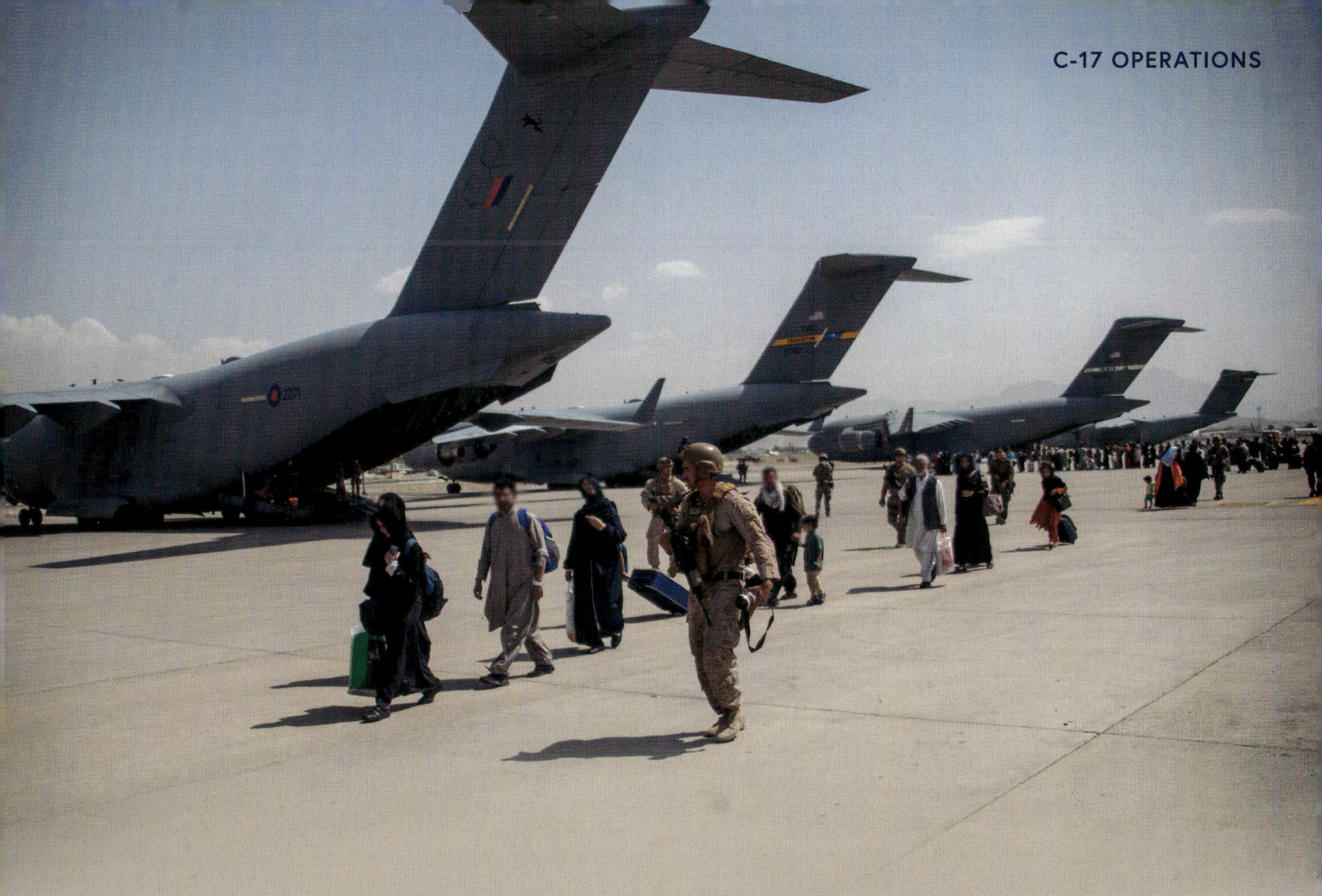

The following day, the aircraft made its first run into Kabul's Hamid Karzai International Airport to deliver enabling personnel and equipment. The rest of 99 Squadron was placed on 24 hours' notice to move.

On August 12, President Biden agreed to recommendations from his military chiefs to send in three more battalions of troops to secure Kabul Airport to allow the evacuation to begin within days. In London, the UK government came to a similar conclusion and dispatched 600 British Paratroopers from 16 Air Assault Brigade to set up an evacuation processing centre near to Kabul airport. A second 99 Squadron C-17 was soon on its way to be in position at RAF Akrotiri for when the evacuation mission reached its peak and the following day it was called forward to Minhad.

At this stage of the crisis, both the British and US governments were still banking on the airport and Kabul city remaining in the hands of the Afghan military. They were planning on a steady stream of civilian charter and scheduled aircraft bringing the vulnerable civilians to safety.

This all changed during the evening of August 14, when Taliban fighters reached the outskirts of the city.

During the early hours of August 14, a C-17 delivered the small British command team of the Joint Force Headquarters (JFH) to Kabul and a contingent of Paratroopers. The scale of the challenge they now faced was rapidly dawning on British commanders and permission was given for RAF C-17s to now carry 250 passengers.

Early on the following day, the first Taliban fighters were spotted inside Kabul, prompting the Afghan President and other senior leaders to head to the airport. More than 40 Afghan aircraft and helicopters took off during the day and headed to safety in Uzbekistan.

The British embassy staff and British passport holders were ordered to head to the airport to be evacuated. Three C-17 missions were made to Kabul, with the first aircraft bringing out 95 civilians. To boost »

RIGHT: 99 Squadron's C-17s flew out two thirds of all the evacuees recovered from Kabul by the RAF during Operation Pitting. MOD/Crown Copyright

BELOW: RAF Police personnel flew on every evacuation flight from Kabul to keep order among civilians and ensure the safety of RAF aircraft. The evacuees proved universally grateful to have been flown to safety by the RAF. MOD/Crown Copyright

the capacity of the 99 Squadron detachment at Minhad, six more C-17 crew were despatched to the airbase from RAF Brize Norton.

Hours after the Afghan leaders had made their escape, tens of thousands of Afghans began swarming into the civilian side of the airport to try to get on any aircraft they could. Once inside the airport, they soon made their way onto the main runways, preventing any aircraft from taking off or landing. US, Turkish and British troops were sent over to try to clear the runway but not before hundreds of refugees had made their way on board at least one USAF C-17 on the morning of August 16. Other refugees tried to climb onto a USAF C-17 as it was making its take-off run, and several Afghans fell to their deaths.

As the maelstrom was unfolding, an RAF Lockheed Martin C-130J Hercules was on the ground at Kabul Airport and the aircraft captain had to 'rev' his propellers to force a passage through the crowds of civilians to get to the runway and take off. An RAF Airbus A400M Atlas on final approach aborted its landing and circled for some time before heading back to Minhad.

No more RAF flights landed in Kabul that day. Allied troops eventually regained control of the airport perimeter and allowed it to re-open for evacuation flights.

The RAF, along with the US and its allies, began surging transport aircraft to the Middle East so the airlift could be stepped up massively. RAF Brize Norton-based airlift squadrons put every available aircraft into the air to join the operation. A third C-17 was dispatched to Minhad on August 17, to join the three RAF C-130Js and four A400M already committed to the operation.

To free up aircraft, spare parts and crew for Operation Pitting, all other air transport tasking was cancelled. The Kabul airlift was now the main effort of 99 Squadron. By August 19, aircraft and plans were in place to begin shuttling C-17s between Minhad and Kabul. Nine C-17 crews were now in Minhad, including personnel from the operational conversion unit, 24 Squadron. Dispensation was given for RAF C-17s to carry 350 passengers. One of the C-17s at Minhad was now declared unserviceable and a replacement aircraft was flown forward from the UK.

On the ground in Kabul, British troops were now getting into their stride processing refugees and, by August 25, 99 Squadron's four C-17s were now flying six missions a day into Kabul.

Refugees were now being seated on the floors of C-17s using safety straps to secure them on the take-off and landing. RAF Tactical Medical Wing nurses and paramedics flew on each aircraft to tend to the needs of the Afghans who had spent days without food and water waiting to gain access to the Kabul airport. RAF Police personnel helped to keep order during the boarding of passengers and RAF Regiment gunners secured the area around C-17s while they were on the ground in Kabul.

The peak of C-17 operations was achieved on August 26, when a 99 Squadron C-17 lifted out of Kabul with 436 refugees, setting a record for passengers carried on a single RAF aircraft.

Tension was high at the airport as the evacuation was nearing its cut-off date at the end of the month set by the Taliban. On August 26, thirteen US military personnel were killed in a suicide bomb attack on one of the airport gates. As the incident was unfolding a C-17 carrying 377 refugees, piloted by 99 Squadron's boss, Wing Commander Kev Latchman, missed a bus carrying civilians, that had accidentally »

British Paratroopers stand guard around the taxi-way of Kabul Airport as an RAF C-17 makes its way to the runway to fly out with another load of evacuees. MoD/Crown Copyright

All of 99 Squadron's aircraft and personnel were back home at RAF Brize Norton by August 31, after concluding Operation Pitting. MoD/Crown Copyright

driven onto the Kabul runway, by 10 feet, averting a potentially disastrous crash. He was later awarded the Air Force Cross for his bravery that day.

The final 99 Squadron evacuation mission was flown on the morning of August 28 and later in the day the last British troops departed from Kabul on two RAF A400Ms. Twenty-four hours later, the last USAF C-17s lifted from Kabul to bring out the final troops of the US 82nd Airborne Division. Already, the C-17 crews of 99 Squadron were heading back to RAF Brize Norton, with the last aircraft returning safely home by August 31.

The British element, Operation Pitting, involved more than 100 RAF sorties into Kabul, including 46 by C-17s, 31 by A400Ms and 24 by C-130Js. As an outsized jet, the C-17 played an outsized role in Operation Pitting. Out of 15,000 civilians and refugees brought out of Kabul by the RAF, 10,121 were carried by 99 Squadron.

The squadron's commitment to Operation Pitting involved six of its eight aircraft, as well as 110 personnel, including 46 pilots, 30 loadmasters, 24 ground engineers and support staff. During the missions, the squadron flew 500 hours, including 280 hours on sorties into Kabul.

LAST FLIGHT OF KITTYHAWK

Operation London Bridge

LEFT: C-17 serial ZZ177 had the honour of carrying Queen Elizabeth II on her final flight into history from Edinburgh to London. MOD/Crown Copyright

When Queen Elizabeth II passed away at her Scottish country estate at Balmoral on September 8, 2022, a well-oiled contingency plan kicked in to return the late monarch to London for her State Funeral.

The Royal Air Force's 99 Squadron played an important role in Operation London Bridge, as the arrangements for the State Funeral were codenamed, with the RAF component of the mission being designated Operation Overstudy.

One of the squadron's Boeing C-17A Globemaster III was tasked to fly the late monarch from Edinburgh, where her body had been Laying-in-State in the city's St Giles Cathedral to RAF Northolt, in west London.

After the Laying-in-State came to an end on

BELOW: A RAF C-17 flew Queen Elizabeth II from Edinburgh International Airport to RAF Northolt, using the official Royal callsign, Kittyhawk, for the last time. MOD Crown Copyright

ABOVE: A bearer party of the RAF Regiment carried Queen Elizabeth II off the RAF C-17 Globemaster at RAF Northolt. MOD/Crown Copyright

Queen Elizabeth II on board, for the last time.

Just over an hour later, the aircraft touched down at RAF Northolt, where Prime Minister Liz Truss and Defence Secretary Ben Wallace were among those waiting for the flight. Another bearer party from the Queen's Colour Squadron, carried the coffin out of the aircraft' hold, past an honour guard from the same RAF Regiment unit.

The late Queen's coffin was then driven in the State Hearse to Buckingham Palace along roads lined with thousands of people who stood in the rain to pay their respects.

The flight went perfectly, with 'Kittyhawk' taking off and landing exactly on time, according to the Operation London Bridge plan. A global television audience watched the event live, and more than six million logged onto the Flightradar25.com aircraft tracking website to follow the progress of the flight. This made it the most tracked flight in history of the website.

The officer commanding 99 Squadron, Wing Commander Will Essex, praised the crew of ZZ177, telling a reporter from the Oxford Mail that, "they carried out the task with absolute perfection and dignity."

Air loadmaster Mark Hamer, who flew in the historic mission, said he had never experienced anything like it in 32 years in the Royal Air Force, commenting. "The gravity of who we had on board and the significance of who we had on board made it a real special day."

the afternoon of September 13, her coffin was taken by hearse to Edinburgh Airport where C-17, serial ZZ177, was waiting to fly it southwards.

A Royal Air Force Regiment Bearer Party drawn from the Queen's Colour Squadron carried the coffin onto the aircraft, past a Guard of Honour from the Royal Regiment of Scotland. The Princess Royal and her husband, Vice Admiral Sir Timothy Laurence, boarded the aircraft for the flight.

As the aircraft began to taxi away, the Guard of Honour gave a final royal salute, while a military band played one verse of the national anthem. During the journey the Scottish version of the Royal Standard that draped the coffin was replaced by the Royal Standard that is used in the remainder of the United Kingdom.

The flight used the traditional Royal callsign 'Kittyhawk', which was used for any military flight with the

Queen Elizabeth II was driven away from RAF Northolt and into history after being safely delivered to the nation's capital by 99 Squadron and the RAF Regiment. MOD/Crown Copyright

C-17 OPERATORS

Global Air Forces

AUSTRALIA

Royal Australian Air Force

Expeditionary operations have been central to Australian defence strategy over the past 30 years. Australia's geographic location means strategic airlift is a must to enable it to move military forces to combat zones in Asia, the Middle East or Europe.

Its reliance on Lockheed C-130 Hercules variants in the 1990s was increasingly seen as major capability gap, so in the early years of this century attention turned to buying the Boeing C-17A Globemaster III. The Australian Department of Defence placed a first $2 billion order to buy four C-17s in March 2006 to meet its requirement for a Responsive Global Airlift (RGA) capability.

LEFT: RAAF C-17s routinely operate with the Australian government's aid agency to deliver humanitarian aid to disaster zones around the world. AusAID

BELOW: Australia was the third international customer for the C-17, taking delivery of its first aircraft in 2026. USAF

Aircraft already under production at Boeing's Long Beach plant in California were diverted to meet the needs of the Royal Australian Air Force (RAAF) and the first aircraft was handed over to its new owners in November 2006, ahead of a ferry flight to Australia the following month. The final aircraft of this initial batch were delivered in 2008.

Two more C-17s were ordered in 2011, the sixth being delivered to the RAAF in November 2012. Another two C-17s were ordered in October 2014, with the final aircraft being delivered in November 2015.

All of the RAAF's C-17s are operated by 36 Squadron, which is based at RAAF Amberley in Queensland. It had operated Lockheed C-130A/H Hercules since 1958, when Australia become the first non-US operator tactical airlifter. Over the next half-century it flew two models of Hercules, the C-130A and C-130H, from at RAAF Richmond, close to Sydney in New South Wales. The squadron, which is part of the RAAF's Air Mobility Group, transferred to RAAF Amberley in 2006, when it took delivery of its first C-17.

Before taking delivery of their aircraft, the RAAF sent an initial cadre of personnel to undergo training with the USAF. In May 2006, a contingent of prospective pilots and load masters, led by the commanding officer designate of 36 Squadron, Wing Commander Linda Corbould,

undertook conversion training with the USAF's C-17 units at Altus AFB and Charleston AFB. Corbould was the first female pilot to command a RAAF squadron. A group of 48 ground technical personnel also received training at Charleston AFB and McChord AFB in September 2006. RAAF C-17 personnel are now trained in Australia.

The RAAF's C-17s are supported under commercial contracts with Boeing and the service has kept its aircraft to the same configuration as the USAF's aircraft to ensure commonality and reduced logistic support costs. This includes the installation of the Large Aircraft Infrared Countermeasures system for protection against surface-to-air missiles.

Since they entered service, the RAAF's C-17s have supported Australian Defence Force (ADF) missions in Afghanistan, Iraq and other locations in the Middle East, as well as training exercises in Australia and the United States.

They have also transported supplies and personnel as part of relief efforts following natural disasters in Australia, Japan, New Zealand and several other countries.

In July 2009, 36 Squadron began flying direct C-17 flights into the major Australian base at Tarin Kot in southern Afghanistan began. At the peak of Australian involvement in the Afghan war in 2013, RAAF C-17s were flying 60 missions, about 330 hours of flight time, each year to Afghanistan. In 2013, 36 Squadron moved 190 vehicles, 1,800 passengers and over 3,600 tonnes of cargo to Afghanistan and conducted 20 aeromedical evacuations. Two Australian C-17 took part in the August 2021 Kabul airlift. In March 2022, RAAF C-17s transported military equipment destined for Ukraine to Rzeszow in Poland in response to the Russian invasion of Ukraine.

RAAF C-17 SERIALS

Royal Australian Air Force	
Serial/Code	Delivered
A41-206/60206	28/11/06
A41-207/60207	11/5/07
A41-208/60208	16/12/07
A41-209/60209	19/1/08
A41-210/110210	14/9/11
A41-211/120211	01/11/12
A41-212/140001	04/9/15
A41-213/140002	24/7/15

ROYAL AUSTRALIAN AIR FORCE AND C-17

Entered Service	2006
Fleet Strength	8
Main Operating Base	RAAF Amberley
Operator	36 Squadron

ABOVE: 36 Squadron flew to Japan in response to the 2011 Tsunami that devastated large parts of the country to deliver humanitarian aid. USAF

BELOW: A RAAF lands at Tarin Kot in southern Afghanistan to resupply the Australian garrison patrolling the remote region. US Army

CANADA
Royal Canadian Air Force

LEFT: A Canadian CC-177 delivers a US Marine Corps HIMARS rocket launcher during a combat training exercise in California. US DoD/Combat Camera

Canada became the third non-US operator of the Boeing C-17A Globemaster when it ordered the strategic airlifter in August 2007 to meet its Future Strategic Airlifter requirement.

During the 1990s, the Air Command of the Canadian Armed Forces leased former Soviet Antonov and Ilyushin transport aircraft to fly large, outsized cargo on overseas missions. In the post 9/11 world, after the 2001 attacks on the United States, the Canadian Department of National Defence began looking to acquire its own heavy lift capability.

In February 2007, Canada finally signed a contract to buy four C-17 aircraft, which were designated CC-177s, which were fitted with the LAIRCM (Large Aircraft Infrared Countermeasures) systems to defeat surface-to-air missile threats.

An initial squadron capability was in place for the arrival of the first C-17 aircraft in on August 8, 2007, at CFB Trenton in Ontario to join 429 (Transport) Squadron, which was part of 8 Wing. The next three aircraft were delivered between October 2007 and April 2008. The unit consisted of approximately 200 members,

BELOW: A Canadian Air Force CC-177 departing from Montreal's Trudeau International Airport after having brought back Canadians following the devastating earthquake in Haiti in 2010. Patcard

ABOVE: RCAF CC-177s are regular visitors to the Royal International Air Tattoo at RAF Fairford.
Adrian Pingstone

BELOW: Canada's CC-177 carry the nation's high-profile branding.
US DoD/Combat Camera

including pilots, loadmasters and technicians.

Canadian pilots flew their first operational mission in the CC-177, to deliver 35 tons of aid to Kingston, Jamaica in the wake of Hurricane Dean in August 2007. Later that month, a CC-177 flew its mission to Kandahar in Afghanistan to deliver supplies to the Canadian contingent in the central Asian country.

On April 14, 2010, a Canadian CC-177 landed for the first time at CFS Alert, the world's most northerly airport. Since then, Canadian CC-177 have been deployed in support of numerous missions worldwide, including Operation Hestia after the 2010 Haiti earthquake and supporting the Canadian mission in Afghanistan. After Typhoon Haiyan hit the Philippines in 2013, CC-177s established an air bridge between the two nations, deploying Canada's disaster relief team and delivering humanitarian supplies and equipment.

In 2014, the Canadian government announced it was to buy a fifth C-17, to be delivered the following year to the then renamed Royal Canadian Air Force.

In August 2021, 429 Squadron played a central role in Operation Aegis, the Canadian contribution to the evacuation of civilians from Kabul in Afghanistan after the fall of the city to the Taliban. The squadron flew nine sorties into Hamid Karzai International Airport from Ali Al Salem Airbase in Kuwait. Out of 3,300 people evacuated from the beleaguered city by the RCAF, 429 flew out 2,784 civilians to safety. One aircraft carried a record 534 refugees. The final contingent of Canadian soldiers was evacuated from Kabul on August 27, by a CC-177.

In the wake of the Russian invasion of Ukraine in February 2022, 429 Squadron was tasked to airlift arms and military equipment to Poland for onward shipment overland into Ukraine to help Kyiv's military.

ROYAL CANADIAN AIR FORCE AND C-17	
Entered Service	2001
Fleet Strength	5
Main Operating Base	CFB Trenton
Operator	429 Squadron

RCAF C-17 SERIALS	
Royal Canadian Air Force	
Serial/Code	Delivered
177701/701	8/8/07
177702/702	18/10/07
177703/703	10/5/08
177704/704	8/5/08
177705/705	30/3/15

HUNGARY/NORTH ATLANTIC TREATY ORGANISATION (NATO)

Heavy Airlift Wing

A shortage of strategic airlift capability was identified as a major shortfall in the NATO's arsenal during the 1990s. In July 2009, NATO activated its multi-national Heavy Airlift Wing to operate the Boeing C-17 Globemaster III strategic transport aircraft.

Since the summer of 2006, several nations worked together to establish the C-17 Strategic Airlift Capability (SAC) consortium. Ten NATO nations (Bulgaria, Estonia, Hungary, Lithuania, the Netherlands, Norway, Poland, Romania, Slovenia, and the United States) and two Partnership for Peace (PfP) nations (Finland and Sweden) eventually signed the SAC Memorandum of Understanding (MOU), which entered into effect on September 23, 2008, formally establishing the SAC Programme.

The SAC MOU established a steering board to exercise overall responsibility for the guidance and oversight of the SAC Programme, and the multinational C-17 unit, the Heavy Airlift Wing (HAW), located at Pápa Airbase (AB), Hungary.

SAC aircraft acquisition, management, and support is executed through the NATO Airlift Management Organization (NAMO), which was established by the North Atlantic Council (NAC) in September 2008. NAMO owns the SAC aircraft and other related equipment and set up the NATO Airlift Management Agency (MAMA) to run things on a daily basis.

HAW personnel and their families began moving to Pápa in October 2008 and training of the multinational HAW crew members and support personnel began in March 2009. In October 2009, NAMO took ownership of the three SAC C-17 aircraft and HAW missions began worldwide.

ABOVE: US paratroopers of the 173rd Airborne Brigade Combat Team board a HAW C-17 during a jump week event at Aviano Air Base in Italy. US Army

RIGHT: The distinctive blue location stripe is carried by the Heavy Air Wing's three C-17s. Jonny Nordling

HAW C-17 – ANNUAL FLIGHT HOUR SHARE

Member state	Flight hours
United States	1000
Sweden	550
The Netherlands	500
Norway	400
Romania	200
Poland	150
Finland	100
Bulgaria	65
Slovenia	60
Hungary	50
Estonia	45
Lithuania	45

Under its Charter, NAMO is responsible for the acquisition, management and logistic support, spare parts and other sustainment activity of the SAC C-17 aircraft and other SAC Programme assets. HAW operations are not, however, under the direct control of NATO's military command structure. SAC nations may determine how best to use their committed flight hours to meet their obligations to NATO, EU, UN or other third parties.

The SAC Programme, over its 30-year life, and including acquisition, support, and operations of three C-17 aircraft, is estimated to cost $5-6 billion US in constant year 2007 prices.

With a total workforce of 35 employees, the NAMA's headquarters have initially collocated within the NATO Maintenance and Supply Agency (NAMSA) headquarters at Capellen, but there are plans eventually to relocate the agency to Pápa AB.

The HAW operational unit will be composed of 135 personnel from the SAC nations. The HAW commander is a USAF officer, and the vice commander is from the Royal Swedish Air Force. Training of the multinational HAW crew members and support personnel began in March 2009.

The United States paid part of its share in the project by providing one aircraft to the SAC Programme. The remaining eleven SAC nations purchased two more C-17 aircraft through NAMA, by using the Foreign Military Sales (FMS) procedures.

All three aircraft and supporting equipment are owned by NAMO. Logistics support is also purchased through NAMA from the United States through FMS. The United States Air Force provided initial qualification training to pilots and loadmasters from SAC nations at Altus AFB in Oklahoma, where all United States C-17 crew members receive their initial training.

With the main operating base located at Pápa AB, Hungary serves as host nation to the HAW. In addition, Hungary serves as the SAC C-17 flag nation and registers the aircraft under Hungarian National Transport Authority airworthiness »

ABOVE: Afghan civilians wait to board a Heavy Airlift Wing C-17 in Kabul during the August 2021 evacuation operation. NATO

BELOW: The Heavy Air Wing's C-17s evacuated 2,299 people from Kabul, Afghanistan in 14 missions. NATO

Pápa AB in Hungary is the main operating base for NATO's Heavy Airlift Wing. NATO

regulations. Hungary made significant national investments at Pápa AB to prepare it for hosting the HAW.

Boeing provides Contractor Logistics Support (CLS) through the C-17 Globemaster III Sustainment Partnership (GSP) and performs contract maintenance for the SAC aircraft. Boeing has approximately 70 personnel located at Pápa AB.

Initial operational capability (IOC) was to be declared by the end of 2009 and full operational capability was declared in 2011, when all the supporting infrastructure and the full complement of personnel were in place.

The construction of the parking ramp was the largest infrastructure development project required at the HAW's Main Operating Base

(MOB). This involved building the 22,000 m2 concrete parking ramp for the three C-17s. The project also included installing a de-icing fluid collection and treatment facility and provisions for a future fuel hydrant system. The total costs were 2.8 million euros.

On September 28, 2009, the HAW conducted its first mission

BELOW LEFT: Afghan refugees disembark from a Heavy Airlift Wing C-17 after being lifted out of Kabul in August 2021. NATO

NATO HEAVY AIRLIFT WING	
Entered Service	2009
Fleet Strength	3
Main Operating Base	Pápa AB, Hungary
Operator	Heavy Airlift Wing

LEFT: The Heavy Airlift Wing supports NATO exercises and operations by carrying cargo around the world every year. NATO

to participate in operations during the Libya crisis.

Over the following decade, HAW aircraft supported NATO exercises in eastern Europe, helped move emergency medical equipment during the COVID 19 pandemic and evacuated civilians from Kabul in August 2021. The Hungary-based C-17s are now a permanent fixture of NATO operations, wherever they might take place.

in support of the International Security Assistance Force (ISAF) in Afghanistan. The first ISAF-related flight by its aircraft delivered materiel to Mazar-e Sharif, to supply Swedish troops in the Afghan theatre.

During 2010, the HAW really got into its stride flying several missions each week to and from Afghanistan to re-supply ISAF troops as well as move in equipment for US units being deployed under the 'surge plan'. Highlights included flying aid missions to the victims of the Haiti earthquake and repatriating the victims of the plane crash in Russia in April 2010 that claimed the life of the Polish President. HAW aircraft were called upon to support the deployment of NATO air units to Italy in March 2011

NATO HAW C-19 SERIALS	
NATO Strategic Airlift Capability	
Serial/Code	Delivered
08-0001/SAC 01	17/7/09
08-0002/SAC 02	17/9/09
08-0003/SAC 03	07/10/09

BELOW: Norwegian troops provided security for Heavy Airlift Wing aircraft during the missions to Kabul. NATO

ABOVE: An 81 Squadron C-17 takes on cargo at Dover AFB during a visit to the United States in November 2020.
USAF

INDIA

Indian Air Force

India is the largest operator of Boeing C-17A Globemaster IIIs outside of the US military, with eleven aircraft currently in service.

After several decades of relying on Soviet and Russian transport aircraft, in the 21st century, the Indian government decided to diversify its sources of military aircraft. This resulted in the Indian military receiving aircraft and helicopters from US companies.

In a bid to rejuvenate its strategic airlift capability, the Indian Air Force (IAF) ordered an initial batch of 10 C-17s in 2012, with an option for up to six more. The first five aircraft were delivered in June 2013 and the remaining five were handed over the following year.

A completely new unit, 81 Squadron, known as the SkyLords, was formed on September 1, 2013, at Hindon Air Force Station, in the state of Uttar Pradesh on the outskirts of the capital, Delhi. An eleventh aircraft was subsequently ordered and finally delivered in August 2019. IAF crews received their initial training on the C-17 at Altus AFB in Oklahoma.

Since entering IAF service, the C-17 has been used extensively to support a wide array of missions, including non-combatant evacuations, delivery of humanitarian aid and special forces missions. The Indian government has dispatched its C-17 on missions across Asia, into the Middle East and Africa.

A major role for the 81 Squadron is the strategic re-deployment of army units across India in response to emergency situations, including to high-altitude bases at Leh and

BELOW: An Indian C-17 departs from RAF Waddington after supporting the deployment of Indian Air Force Mirage 2000s during Exercise Cobra Warrior.
Alan Wilson

ABOVE: The crew of an Indian Air Force C-17 during a stage over at Dover AFB in the United States. USAF

for earthquake victims in Turkey and Syria.

Perhaps the most daring mission flown by the 81 Squadron involved the delivery of a contingent of Indian Navy Marine Commando Force (MCF or MARCOS) into the sea off the coast of Somalia to rescue the crew of the bulk carrier MV *Ruen* being held by pirates. An IAF C-17 executed a precision airdrop of two Combat Rubberised Raiding Craft along with a platoon of MARCOS commandos close to the pirate-held ship, allowing them to board the vessel, release its 17-strong crew and capture 35 pirates.

INDIAN AIR FORCE AND C-17

Entered Service	2013
Fleet Strength	1
Main Operating Base	Hindon Air Station
Operator	81 Squadron

Thoise. The IAF first used the C-17 was transport an infantry battalion's equipment to Port Blair on Andaman Islands in July 2013.

The span of operations included flying oxygen canister to medical facilities across India during the COVID-19 pandemic in 2020.

Evacuations of civilians in war zones took place in Yemen in 2015 and Sudan in 2016. A major operation was launched by 81 Squadron during the fall of Kabul in August 2021, when Indian diplomats, as well as Indian and local civilians were flown out of the Afghan capital, via Tajikistan.

Long range missions have also been flown to Rwanda to support Indian peacekeepers serving with the United Nations in the central African region.

In February 2023, an IAF C-17 delivered humanitarian aid packages

IAF C-17 SERIALS

Indian Air Force

Serial	Delivered
CB-8001	22/1/13
CB-8002	22/7/13
CB-8003	20/8/13
CB-8004	19/10/13
CB-8005	22/11/13
CB-8006	21/11/14
CB-8007	12/12/14
CB-8008	29/10/14
CB-8009	22/7/14
CB-8010	10/9/14
CB-8011	23/8/19

RIGHT: IAF C-17 aircraft executed a precision airborne drop of two Combat Rubberised Raiding Craft (CRRC) boats, along with Indian Navy MARCOS commandoes in the Arabian Sea in a bid to rescue the crew of bulk carrier vessel MV *Ruen*, which had been hijacked by Somali pirates near Yemeni island of Socotra recently. Government of India

STATE OF KUWAIT

Kuwait Air Force

The oil rich Gulf state ordered its first of two Boeing C-17A Globemaster III strategic airlifters in 2010, in a deal reported to be worth $693 million, which also included training and logistic support. A second aircraft was subsequently ordered.

Kuwaiti crews were initially trained on the aircraft by USAF and Boeing instructors at Altus AFB, in Oklahoma, before the first aircraft was delivered in February 2014, sporting a unique white and grey livery. The second aircraft followed in September 2014. Kuwait C-17 crews underwent a month of "seasoning" training with the USAF's 17th Airlift Squadron at Joint Base Charleston in South Carolina, to give them hands-on experience of using the aircraft in tactical situations. This included ground, simulator, and flight training.

Kuwait's two C-17s are operated by 42 Squadron, which is based at Abdul Al Mubarak Air Base on the military side of Kuwait International airport.

The stated reason for Kuwait buying the aircraft was to allow strategic air transport and humanitarian missions to be flown to boost the

LEFT: Kuwait Air Force pilots train in a C-17 flight deck simulator at Joint Base Lewis-McChord in Washington State in April 2025. USAF

LEFT: Kuwait Air Force personnel unload an AH-64E Apache from a C-17 at Ali Al Salem Air Base in Kuwait in July 2021. USAF

KUWAITI AIR FORCE AND C-17	
Role	Airlift
Entered Service	2013
Fleet Strength	2
Main Operating Base	Abdul Al Mubarak Air Base
Operator	42 Squadron

influence of the small Gulf country. After the 2023 Turkish earthquake, the Kuwaiti C-17s played a prominent role in delivering aid to the victims of the disaster.

The Kuwaiti C-17s are regularly spotted around the world picking up cargo for the country's armed forces, including delivering AH-64 Apache attack helicopters from Boeing's factory in Mesa, Arizona, to Kuwait.

KAF C-17 SERIALS	
Serial/Code	Delivered
KAF 342/130001	13/2/14
KAF 343/130002	26/9/14

BELOW: A Kuwait Air Force C-17 departs Prestwick in November 2015 during a transit across the Atlantic. Mark Harkin

STATE OF QATAR

Qatar Emiri Air Force

The oil and gas rich Gulf emirate operates one of the largest Boeing C-17A Globemaster III fleets outside the US, with eight aircraft in its inventory.

Qatar's rulers have emerged as major players in Middle East affairs over the past decade and launched a build-up its air force to both defend their home territory and project influence around the region.

Over the past twenty years the Qatar Emiri Air Force (QEAF) has undergone a rapid expansion, including becoming a significant operator of the C-17. The first Qatari aircraft was delivered in August 2009 and the second followed a month later. Two more were delivered in 2012. A second batch of aircraft were delivered in 2016.

All the aircraft are operated by the QEAF's 10 Squadron, based at Al Udeid Airbase outside of the country's capital, Doha. The QEAF C-17 unit maintains very close relations with the USAF and Boeing for the training and maintenance of their aircraft. Qatari aircrew and maintenance personnel receive training in the United States and its aircraft are serviced at USAF bases under the Boeing-led global sustainment solution. Al Udeid Airbase is also the home of the USAF region airlift hub in the Gulf region, so USAF and QEAF personnel work side by side on their C-17s at the large base.

Qatar bought its C-17s to assist with "humanitarian aid, disaster relief and peacekeeping missions" but over the past 15 years they have been seen flying in some unexpected places. In 2012, QEAF C-17s were reported to have flown arms from Libya to rebels in Syria, via Turkish air bases. In August 2021, QEAF C-17s flew Qatari diplomats to Kabul in the days after US troops left Afghanistan to establish contacts with the new Taliban rules of the central Asian country.

QATARI EMIRI AIR FORCE AND C-17	
Role	Airlift
Entered Service	2009
Fleet Strength	8
Main Operating Base	Al Udeid Airbase
Operator	10 Squadron

QEAF C-17 SERIALS	
Serial/Code	Delivered
A7-MAA/80201	11/8/09
A7-MAB/80202	11/9/09
A7-MAC/120203	09/10/12
A7-MAE/120204	10/12/12
A7-MAM/140005	14/3/16
A7-MAN/140006	07/3/16
A7-MAO/140009	26/5/16
A7-MAP/140010	26/2/16

ABOVE: Qatari Emiri Air Force C-17s are routinely seen around the world to collect cargo. This aircraft visited Toulouse-Blagnac Airport (LFBO) in France in October 2014. Laurent Errera

LEFT: One of the QEAF's C-17s is painted in the colours of the Gulf State's national airline to allow it to pass as a civilian aircraft and visit a wider range of airports around the world. USAF

UNITED ARAB EMIRATES

United Arab Emirates Air Force

The United Arab Emirates has emerged as an important military power in the Middle East on the back of a major expansion of its armed forces, including its air force.

US Aerospace companies have played a key part in this build up, with Boeing starting deliveries of eight Boeing C-17A Globemaster aircraft in May 2011.

At the official handover ceremony at Boeing's Long Beach factory, the UAE Ambassador to the USA, Al Otaiba, said the aircraft were intended to enhance UAE missions to promote "regional peace and stability."

Later in 2011, the UAE Air Force (UAEAF) took delivery of three more C-17s and two more aircraft followed in 2012. A second top-up batch was subsequently ordered, and these aircraft were handed over in 2016.

15th Strategic Airlift Squadron operates the aircraft from the military ramp at Zayed International Airport, just outside the UAE's capital Abu Dhabi. The USAF and Boeing continue to provide training and logistic support for the UAEAF C-17s, which are supported via Boeing's global sustainment programme.

Since they arrived in the UAEAF service, the C-17s have reportedly flown missions to Libya and Yemen to assist allies of the UAE government. UAEAF C-17s also flew missions to Kabul in August 2021 to evacuate civilians from the city. In 2024, UAEAF C-17s took part in the air dropping of humanitarian aid to the war-torn Palestinian enclaves in Gaza. They have also been spotted in China providing logistic support for UAEAF fighter jets taking part in joint exercises with the People's Liberation Army Air Force.

UNITED ARAB EMIRATES AIR FORCE AND C-17	
Entered Service	2001
Fleet Strength	8
Main Operating Base	Zayed International Airport
Operator	15th Strategic Airlift Squadron

UAE C-17 SERIALS	
Serial	Delivered
1223	10/5/11
1224	10/6/11
1225	28/7/11
1226	26/9/11
1227	14/5/12
1228	13/6/12
1229	26/5/15
1230	29/6/15

ABOVE: UAEAF C-17s flew to Kabul's Hamid Karzai International Airport, Kabul, Afghanistan to evacuate civilians in August 2021. US Marine Corps

BELOW: A United Arab Emirate C-17 departs from Marine Corps Air Ground Combat Center, Twentynine Palms in California in February 2022, during a joint training exercise with the US Marine Corps. US Marine Corps

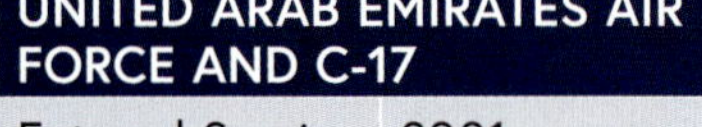

KEY.AERO
The World's Fastest Growing Aviation Website

UNITED KINGDOM

Royal Air Force

Britain's global reach is underpinned by its fleet of eight Boeing C-17A Globemaster III strategic airlifters, which were first handed over to the RAF in May 2001.

The C-17A filled a gap in RAF capability that was created by the retirement of its Shorts Belfast strategic airlifters in 1976. In the 1998 Strategic Defence Review it was decided to acquire a strategic airlift capability, to allow outsized cargos such as Chinook heavy lift helicopters, or Warrior armoured vehicles, to be flown to war zones on the far side of the world.

A competition was launched to select the best solution and eventually it was decided to lease four C-17As from Boeing, at a cost of £100 million a year. The four aircraft were delivered to the RAF's 99 Squadron at RAF Brize Norton in the summer of 2001 in time to help deliver British peacekeeping troops to Macedonia to join NATO's mission to stabilise the country.

After the 9/11 attacks on New York and Washington DC in 2001, the RAF C-17s were to the fore delivering British troops and their equipment to Afghanistan. A task force of Royal Marines and its supporting Chinook helicopters were flown to Afghanistan by 99 Squadron in the spring of 2002.

When NATO launched an extended mission in Afghanistan in 2006, Britain expanded its troop contingent in the Central Asian country to a brigade strength. This required a major airlift operation by 99 Squadron. Soon British troops were

ROYAL AIR FORCE AND C-17	
Entered Service	2001
Fleet Strength	8
Main Operating Base	RAF Brize Norton
Operator	99 Squadron

RIGHT: 99 Squadron's Puma badge was selected because the squadron's first aircraft, the Airco DH.9 was powered by Puma engines. The cat was chosen for independence and tenacity while the black colour signifies it original night-bombing role. Tim Ripley

BELOW: The RAF has operated the C-17 since May 2021, supporting global missions by the British armed forces. Tim Ripley

locked in heavy fighting and the RAF airlift was expanded dramatically with C-17As making flights back and forth to Afghanistan two or three times a week.

In 2004, the Ministry of Defence decided to buy out the leases of the four original aircraft. Two years later, an order for four more aircraft was placed with Boeing to bring the fleet up to eight aircraft, with the first aircraft being delivered in 2008. The final two aircraft were handed over in 2010 and 2012.

This allowed the RAF to sustain its 'air bridge' to Afghanistan out to 2014 when British troops finished their combat mission in Helmand province. As well as flying troops,

A RAF C-17 Globemaster arrived in Egypt in November 2023 to deliver British humanitarian aid to civilians in Gaza. *MoD/Crown Copyright*

RAF C-17 SERIALS

Serial	Delivered
ZZ171	17/5/01
ZZ172	12/6//01
ZZ173	31/7/01
ZZ174	23/8/01
ZZ175	12/2/08
ZZ176	11/6/08
ZZ177	16/11/10
ZZ178	18/5/12

ammunition and supplies back and forth to Afghanistan, 99 Squadron held a C-17 fitted out for casualty evacuation which was held on alert ready to fly out to Afghanistan to bring home seriously wounded British soldiers. The C-17s also had to perform the solemn duty of flying home fallen British soldiers.

99 Squadron has a long history as an air transport unit, stretching back to 1945 when it was reformed to fly the Avro York. It had originally

formed in 1917 as one of the first Royal Flying Corps bomber squadrons. After World War One it relocated to India, where it took part in fighting against tribes in the Northwest Frontier region. During this time, it became known as the 99 (Madras Presidency) Squadron. In World War Two it flew Vickers Wellington and Consolidated Liberator bombers in Europe and Southeast Asia.

BELOW: A 99 Squadron C17 aircraft taking off from RAF Brize Norton to deliver supplies to French on counter-terrorist duty in the Central African Republic in 2013. *MoD/Crown Copyright*

UNITED STATES AIR FORCE
USAF C-17 UNITS

The United States Air Force assigns its Boeing C-17A Globemaster III airlifters to a variety of types of units, across its active duty and reserve components. The basic C-17 unit is the airlift squadron, which usually have between eight and 13 aircraft assigned to them, as well as aircrew and support personnel.

Airlift squadrons are assigned to a mix of wings, which control multiple squadrons. There are two main types of wings: airlift and air mobility. Airlift wings consist of purely airlift squadrons. Air mobility wings usually combine airlift and air-to-air refuelling squadrons. At locations outside the Continental United States, C-17 squadrons are often combined into multi-role wings with units flying fighters, strike or surveillance aircraft. These are just termed wings.

Generally, C-17 squadrons operate as independent units with their own aircraft to allow them to deploy overseas and operate for short periods. For longer term deployments, support personnel and equipment can be assigned from specialist operations, aeromedical evacuation, aerial port, maintenance, contingency response and civil engineering squadrons.

During extended operational missions, deployed airlift squadrons and supporting units are often formed into expeditionary airlift squadrons or wings for the duration of their deployment. They date the numerical designation of the unit that provides the most aircraft or personnel.

At a number of major bases, where active duty and reserve component units are co-located, they draw aircraft from a common pool that is maintained centrally to enhance maintenance and logistic efficiency. These wings are termed 'associate' units to signify their blended nature. They allow reserve aircrew and maintenance personnel to be fully integrated with their active-duty counterparts for both routine on-base activity and during overseas deployments.

USAF C-17 GLOBAL FOOTPRINT	
Continental USA – Air Mobility Command/ US Air Force Reserve/Air National Guard	**PAA**
Travis AFB, California	13
McChord AFB, Washington	42
McGuire AFB, New Jersey	13
Edwards AFB, California	1?
Dover AFB, Delaware	13
Charleston AFB, South Carolina	40
Wright-Patterson AFB, Ohio	9
March ARB, California	13
Altus AFB, Oklahoma	13
Pittsburgh Air Reserve Station, Pennsylvania	8
Stewart ANGB, New York	8
Charlotte Air National Guard Base, North Carolina	8
Memphis ANGB, Tennessee	8
Shepherd Field ANGB, West Virginia	8
Allen C. Thompson Field ANGB, Mississippi	12
Pacific Air Forces	
Hickam AFB, Hawaii	8
Elmendorf AFB, Alaska	8

Note
AFB: Air Force Base
ANGB: Air National Guard Base
PAA: Primary Aircraft Authorized (assignd to airbase)

BELOW: USAF air mobility wings comprise squadrons operating different types of airlifters and air-to-air refuelling tankers.
USAF

3RD WING

Joint Base Elmendorf-Richardson, Alaska

Dedicated heavy airlift support for US military forces based in Alaska is provided by the 517th Airlift Squadron at Joint Base Elmendorf-Richardson.

The unit is part of the 3rd Wing. This is the focus of the USAF presence in the 49th State of the Union, which is less than 90 kilometres from the Russian coast. Alaska's northern shoreline is rich in oil and other minerals but for much of the year is shrouded in snow and ice.

The 517th Airlift squadron operated the Lockheed C-130H Hercules up until June 2007 when the first Boeing C-17A Globemaster III arrived. Aircraft 00-0169 was named 'Spirit of Denali', after the highest mountain in Alaska and North America, which was formerly Mount McKinlay up to 2015.

By November 2007, all the squadron's eight aircraft had arrived in Alaska and it started to operate in support of US military operations in the Indo-Pacific regions and further afield. These aircraft were initially transferred from McChord AFB in Washington State.

The squadron can trace its history back to 1941, when it was activated as the 7th Transport Squadron flying Douglas C-47 Skytrain transport aircraft. It operated in Burma and the Mediterranean in World War Two. In the Cold War period it supported early warning radar sites in the Arctic and served in Vietnam.

ABOVE: The 517th Airlift Squadron operates C-17s across the Arctic Circle to support US military forces based in 49th State. USAF

Joint Base Elmendorf-Richardson in Alaska is home to a combined force of combat, airlift, support and surveillance aircraft. USAF

517th Airlift Squadron

15TH WING

Joint Base Pearl Harbor–Hickam, Hawaii

Hickam is one of the USAF's most historic airfields, thanks to its role in the December 7, 1941, Japanese surprise attack on Pearl Harbor naval base, which brought the United States into World War Two. The airfield, on the island of Oahu in the state of Hawaii, suffered heavy damage during the Japanese onslaught but it was soon back in action and became the hub for US air operations in the central Pacific region.

The airfield continues to play an important role in the US power projection operations in the Pacific theatre, hosting the headquarters of US Pacific Air Forces. Hawaii's location in the centre of the Pacific means it is a key transit point for aircraft heading to or returning from Japan, South Korea, Philippines, Southeast Asia and Australia. Daniel K. Inouye International Airport is collocated with the US military airfield. In 2010, Hickham AFB was renamed Joint Base Pearl Harbor–Hickam as part of a drive to reduce administrative costs by merging the USAF base with the nearby US Navy base.

The 15th Wing was formed in 2010, out of the old 15th Airlift Wing, and brought together airlift, fighter and air-to-air refuelling aircraft under a single command.

Boeing C-17A Globemaster IIIs first arrived on Hawaii in February 2006 when aircraft 05-5146 landed at Hickam AFB to allow the 535th Airlift Squadron to begin converting to the new airlifter. The aircraft bore the name, 'Spirit of Hawaii – Ke Aloha', in honour the 50th State.

By July 2006, all the 535th Airlift Squadron's eight aircraft had arrived at Hickham AFB. Since then, it has supported USAF airlift operations across the Pacific region and further afield. The squadron is supported by its reserve component associate aviators from the 204th Airlift Squadron of the Hawaii Air National Guard.

ABOVE: The historic Hickam Field is still in use today and its proximity to Pearl Harbor naval base made it a prime target for Japanese bombers on December 7, 1941. The USAF airfield now shares runways and other facilities with Oahu's main civilian airport. Coolcaesar

LEFT: Air-to-air refuelling is essential to allow the Hawaii-based C-17 535th Airlift Squadron project US air power across the Pacific region. USAF

The last C-17 delivered to the 15th Wing is named, 'Spirit of Kamehameha-Imua', after the historic war cry of ancient King of Hawaii. USAF

The 535th Airlift Squadron was formed in 1943 as a fighter training unit and was reformed in 1952 as an airlift unit to support the Korean War. It later flew airlift mission across Southeast Asia during the Vietnam war before being disbanded in 1975. In 2005, the squadron was reactivated as part of the fielding of the C-17, and it was assigned a key role supporting US operations in the Pacific region.

SUBORDINATE UNIT

535th Airlift Squadron

As well as flying its own missions around the Pacific, the 15th Wing routinely hosts and supports state-side C-17 aircraft that are transiting across the Pacific. It provides maintenance support for C-17s that need to refuel, crew rest and maintenance.

BELOW: 15th Wing C-17s have to share the Hickham runway with a variety of USAF, US Navy and visiting allied aircraft, which stop off on Hawaii during transits of the Pacific. USAF

60TH AIR MOBILITY WING

Travis AFB, California

RIGHT: The 'Spirit of Travis' was the last C-17 delivered to the Californian base in 2007. USAF

BELOW: Travis AFB in California is known as the 'Gateway to the Pacific'. USAF

ABOVE: Migrants were deported to central America from Travis AFB in a C-17 on the orders of US President Donald Trump in January 2025. USAF

Travis AFB is located on the southwestern edge of the Sacramento Valley and is known as the 'Gateway to the Pacific' because it handles more cargo and passenger traffic through its airport than any other military air terminal in the United States. It boasts a work force of around 7,000 active USAF military personnel, 3,000 Air Force Reserve personnel and 3,600 civilian staff.

Travis AFB has been home to airlift units since 1958 and as the Vietnam war escalated its resident unit was designated the 60th Military Airlift Wing (MAW), flying the Lockheed C-141 Starlifter and Lockheed C-5 Galaxy. In 1969, the US Air Force Reserve 349th MAW was stood up at the base as one of the first associate units to share aircraft, aircrews and maintenance support.

SUBORDINATE UNIT

21st Airlift Squadron

In 1994, the 60th MAW was redesignated the 60th Air Mobility Wing (AMW) to reflect its new multi-role nature, flying C-5, C-141 and McDonnell Douglas KC-10 Extender air-to-air refuelling tankers.

In August 2006, the first Boeing C-17A Globemaster III arrived at Travis AFB when aircraft serial 05-5154, named the 'Spirit of Solano' after the country where it is based, touched down to allow the standing up of the 21st Airlift Squadron. The squadron has 13 aircraft assigned to it.

The 60th AMW currently also boasts a squadron of C-5M airlifters and Boeing KC-46 Pegasus air-to-air refuelling tankers.

The 21st Transport Squadron was originally formed in Australia in 1942 and operated in the New Guinea theatre. It served in the Korean War and then flew tactical airlift missions in the Vietnam conflict, including resupplying the besieged US Marine outpost at Khe Sanh in 1968.

It returned stateside in 1993 from Japan and traded its Lockheed C-130s in for C-141 and then C-5. The arrival of the C-17 in 2006, saw the start of a new era for the 21st Airlift Squadron, which saw it operate in support of US forces in the Middle East and Afghanistan.

By combining airlift and tanker aircraft on a single base, the 21st Airlift Squadron is able to routinely practice using air-to-air refuelling for long range missions.

BELOW: Fire trucks say farewell to the 60th AMW's commanding officer Colonel Jeffrey Nelson in June 2006 by spraying his aircraft in water. USAF

A 62nd Airlift Wing C-17s takes part in a security force exercise while deployed to Aviano Airbase in Italy. USAF

62ND AIRLIFT WING

Joint Base Lewis-McChord, Washington

From its position on the US west coast, in Washington State, Joint Base Lewis-McChord is ideally placed to support airlift operations across the length and breadth of the Pacific region.

In 1947, the then McChord Field took on the airlift role that continues to this day. In the 1960s the first Lockheed C-141 Starlifters arrived, and they played an important role in the Vietnam war.

Over the decade, the 62nd Troop Carrier Wing transitioned to being the 62nd Air Transport Wing and the 62nd Military Airlift Wing. It became the 62nd Airlift Wing in 1991 on the formation of Air Mobility Command.

McChord has a long association with the Boeing C-17A Globemaster III, with the first aircraft arriving at the airbase in July 1999. It was the second airbase to receive the C-17. The 'Spirit of McChord', aircraft 98-0052, was delivered to the 7th Airlift Squadron. Deliveries to the other squadrons at McChord quickly followed over the next five years and they replaced all the C-141s. One of the C-17 squadrons subsequently disbanded in 2016.

US Air Force Reserve aviators of the 446th Airlift Wing (Associate)

BELOW: McChord AFB is the largest C-17 base on the US West coast, boasting seven USAF and US Air Force Reserve flying squadrons and a fleet of 42 C-17s. USAF

work closely with their active-duty counterparts, including sharing their fleet of 42 C-17s based at McChord. With its three active duty and three reserve squadrons, McChord is the largest C-17 unit on the US West coast.

McChord-based C-17s were some of the first to deploy to the Middle East in September and October 2001 to support the US invasion of Afghanistan in the aftermath of the 9/11 attacks.

The base has hosted the Air Mobility Rodeo competition, which tests USAF and allied airlift personnel in their core skills. The 62nd Airlift Wing's C-141s regularly flew Operation Deep Freeze to resupply US Antarctic Survey bases on the southern continent and this mission subsequently passed to the new C-17s when they arrived at McChord.

ABOVE: Projecting airpower across the Pacific region is a key mission of the 62nd Airlift Wing. USAF

SUBORDINATE UNITS

4th Airlift Squadron

7th Airlift Squadron

8th Airlift Squadron

10th Airlift Squadron (active 2003–2016)

57th Weapons Squadron

In late 2004 and early 2005, 62nd Airlift Wing delivered emergency relief supplies throughout Southeast Asia in response to the tsunami that struck in December 2004.

Aircraft from McChord were heavily involved in Operation Allies Refuge to evacuate civilians from the Afghan capital Kabul, after the fall of the city to Taliban in August 2021.

Since 2017, the 57th Weapons Squadron has been based at McChord. It reports to Air Combat Command and provides graduate level training in advanced tactical skills, such as combat parachuting and austere air strip operations. The squadron did not possess aircraft of its own but uses C-17s sourced from across Air Mobility Command, to allows it to conduct two classes a year.

BELOW: McChord's C-17s are recognisable by the green coloured name stripes on their tail fins. USAF

305TH AIR MOBILITY WING

Joint Base McGuire-Dix-Lakehurst, New Jersey

The New Jersey airbase was first built in 1941 and was renamed McGuire AFB in 1948 after it re-opened under the control of the newly formed US Air Force.

It was named after Major Thomas B. McGuire, a Medal of Honor recipient, and the second leading US fighter ace of World War Two, with 38 kills to his credit. From 2009, the facility was renamed Joint Base McGuire-Dix-Lakehurst.

The base soon became a major airlift hub and was dubbed the USAF's 'Gateway to the East'.

The main Air Mobility Command unit on the base is the 305th Air Mobility Wing, which files the Boeing C-17A Globemaster III airlifter and Boeing KC-46 Pegasus air-to-air refuelling tankers. It shares its 13 C-17 aircraft with the US Air Force Reserve 514th Air Mobility Wing (Associate).

Joint Base McGuire-Dix-Lakehurst in New Jersey is home to the 305th Air Mobility Wing. It was formally known as McGuire AFB. USAF

A McGuire C-17 touches down at an airbase in the Middle East, demonstrating the global reach of the 305th Air Mobility Wing. USAF

The 6th Airlift Squadron is the oldest airlift squadron in the USAF, serving with distinction since October 1, 1933. In September 2004, it received its first C-17, aircraft 03-315, named the 'Spirit of New Jersey' to replace its old Lockheed C-141B Starlifters. It was the last active-duty unit to fly the veteran C-141.

Since converting to the C-17, the squadron has been heavily tasked to fly resupply missions for US forces in Iraq and Afghanistan, staging through air bases in Europe to reach forward operating locations across the Middle East.

Major humanitarian relief operations include responding to the Indian Ocean Tsunami in 2004 and Hurricane Katrina in 2005, as well as participating in Operation Allies Refuge, the evacuation of civilians from Kabul.

For six consecutive months, from October 1, 2024, to March 31, 2025, it distinguished itself as the most heavily tasked C-17 squadron in the USAF, executing more missions, sorties, flight hours, cargo deliveries, and passenger movements than any other C-17 squadron during that timeframe.

These efforts included the supply of major munitions and materiel movements to Europe to support Ukraine's defence. Additionally, its delivered Sikorsky MH-60R Sea Hawk helicopters to the Indian Navy to enhance anti-submarine and anti-mine capabilities, and a THAAD missile defence system was deployed to US Central Command area of responsibility in response to rising missile threats from Iran and Houthi forces.

The squadron was also tasked to support international visits by US President Joe Biden to Berlin, the Asia-Pacific Economic Cooperation Summit in Lima, Peru, the Group of 20 Summit in Brazil, and an historic first presidential visit to Angola.

A 305th Air Mobility Wing's C-17 flew Vice President Joe Biden to Sather Air Base in Iraq in August 2010 to visit US troops in the Middle East country. USAF

SUBORDINATE UNIT

6th Airlift Squadron

BELOW: The 305th and 514th Air Mobility Wing's share a joint fleet of 12 C-17 airlifters. USAF

Dover AFB is home to C-5 and C-17s of the 436th Airlift Wing. USAF

436TH AIRLIFT WING

Dover AFB, Delaware

Dover AFB is the busiest and largest US Air Force air freight terminal, and its passenger terminal moves over 100,000 individuals each year. It has played a key role on all of America's overseas campaigns over the past 35 years, acting as an important launch point for transport aircraft heading out across the Atlantic.

Since 2001, the airbase has been the receiving site for the remains of fallen American military personnel, killed in action in Iraq and Afghanistan.

The 436th Airlift Wing, also known as the 'Eagle Wing', operates Boeing C-17A Globemaster IIIs and Lockheed Martin C-5M Galaxy, sharing these aircraft with the 512th Airlift Wing (Associate) of the US Air Force Reserve. Its 3rd Airlift Squadron is assigned 13 C-17s, with aircraft 06-6165, which is named 'Spirit of the Constitution' in honour of Delaware's historic role as the first state of the Union, arriving at the base in June 2007.

Since its arrival at Dover AFB in 1973, the 3rd Airlift Squadron has

BELOW: The 436th Airlift Wing's C-17s sport the unit's distinctive light blue base identification strip on their tail fin. USAF

earned a reputation as one of Air Mobility Command's most proficient units. Its motto is "Third but First!".

The squadron's C-17s routinely fly airlift missions throughout the world, projecting global reach to more than 90 countries on six continents including Asia, Africa, Australia, Europe, North America, and South America.

It flew its first C-17 mission in support of Operation Iraqi Freedom on May 23, 2008, less than 24-hours after the 3rd Airlift Squadron completed its conversion to the new aircraft. In August 2008, the squadron became the first C-17 unit to fly to Georgia in the Caucasus, to deliver humanitarian supplies in the wake of Russia's invasion. During June 2009, the 3rd Airlift Squadron became the first flying unit from the 436th Airlift Wing to deploy, as a whole, to the Middle East in support of Operation Iraqi Freedom.

In April 2015, the wing dispatched the first USAF aircraft, a C-17, carrying cargo and personnel for humanitarian aid following the earthquake in Nepal. The plane carried a United States Agency for International Development Disaster Assistance Response Team, the Fairfax County, Virginia Urban Search and Rescue Team and 45 tons of cargo.

In January 2023, the 3rd Airlift Squadron spearheaded the testing of a new C-17 combat offloading procedure known as Method C. This allows aircrews to safely deliver palletised cargo off the aft ramp without the use of forklifts or other types of aircraft cargo handling vehicles.

A normal C-17 Method A combat offload consists of opening the cargo door, unlocking a pallet, then using inertia to slide the pallet off the ramp. With Method C, a pallet will be moved to the ramp then locked into the rail system and attached to a winch. The ramp is then lowered and angled to 12 inches off the ground, allowing the pallet to be winched out slowly. This will allow the pallet to slide down the ramp and be gently lowered to the ground. Finally, the winch is disconnected before the aircraft taxis forward allowing the pallet to completely drop to the ground.

ABOVE: A 436th Airlift Wing C-17 during air-to-air refuelling with a KC-10 tanker aircraft. USAF

BELOW: The Method C combat offload technique was trialled by Dover AFB's C-17s. USAF

3rd Airlift Squadron

437TH AIRLIFT WING

Joint Base Charleston, South Carolina

The then Charleston AFB was the first USAF installation to receive the Boeing C-17A Globemaster when aircraft 59-1192, 'Spirit of Charleston', was delivered on June 14, 1993. By January 1995, 17th Airlift Squadron declared initial operational capability as the first frontline C-17 unit.

The South Carolina airbase had served as an airlift installation since 1953 and by 1966, the 437th Military Airlift Wing was the main unit at the base. It flew the C-141 aircraft until the first C-17s started to arrive. The 315th Military Airlift Wing (Associate) of the US Air Force Reserve stood up at Charleston AFB in 1973.

Since 1993, the airbase has been the West coast hub of C-17 operations and it currently hosts three active duty and three reserve airlift squadrons, which share a fleet of 40 aircraft. From 1991 it was re-titled the 437th Airlift Wing after the formation of Air Mobility Command. In 2010,

the airbase was merged with the US Navy's Naval Support Activity Charleston to create Joint Base Charleston.

Its location in South Carolina, close to the bases of the 82nd and 101st Airborne Division, as well as the highly secret Joint Special

ABOVE: A C-17 of the 437th Airlift Wing over flies the Arthur Ravenel Bridge near Charleston, South Carolina.

LEFT: Aircraft and crews are held on 24/7/265 alert at Charleston AFB to respond to short notice tasking from the Joint Chiefs of Staff.
USAF

LEFT: A C-17 loads a batch of ammunition before airlifting it overseas from Joint Base Charleston. USAF

Operation Command (JSOC), mean the 437th Wing is often in the forefront of US Army deployments into foreign combat zones. Its crews are trained to carry out mass parachute drops by the 82nd Airborne and regularly exercise this on drop zones around Fort Bragg in North Carolina.

In September 2001, the 17th Airlift Squadron was the first C-17 unit to deploy to the Middle East in the aftermath of the 9/11 attacks. It formed the core of an expeditionary airlift squadron at Al Udeid Airbase in Qatar, flying missions around the Middle East and eventually into Afghanistan. These missions included airdropping food and equipment to US Special Operations Force teams in Afghanistan, as well dropping humanitarian aid to tribes fighting the Taliban.

To assist these types of deployments, a special detachment of C-141 highly trained crews formed at Charleston AFB in 1980. These so-called Special Operations Low Level II (SOLL II) crews are trained to land on austere airstrips at night using night vision goggles. In 2000, the first C-17 SOLL II crews stood up and they played an important role landing the first US Marines in Afghanistan in November 2001. This role was first held by the 16th Airlift Squadron, but the specialist skills have now been spread around the other two C-17 units of the wing.

SOLL II C-17 crews are held on 24 hours alert, seven days a week, to respond to short-notice National Command Authority taskings, that are issued direct by the Joint Chiefs of Staff. As well as airlifting the elite troops of JSOC to crisis zone, the alert aircraft are also routinely tasked to support presidential visits, national emergencies and humanitarian crisis.

SUBORDINATE UNITS

14th Airlift Squadron
15th Airlift Squadron
16th Airlift Squadron
17th Airlift Squadron (active 1993–2015)

BELOW: With 40 C-17 airlifters at the airbase, Joint Base Charleston is the home of the second largest C-17 wing in the USAF. USAF

97TH AIR MOBILITY WING

Altus AFB, Oklahoma

LEFT: Air-to-air refuelling is key skill for C-17 pilots to learn. USAF

The 97th Air Mobility Wing (AMW) is assigned to Air Education and Training Command and is the main 'schoolhouse' for the Boeing C-17A Globemaster III and other Air Mobility Command aircraft.

All prospective C-17 pilots, co-pilots and loadmasters from the active duty and reserve component undergo conversion training to the aircraft at the Oklahoma air base.

C-17 training started at Altus AFB in the mid-1990s after the 58th Airlift Squadron stood up as the home of all aircrew training on the new aircraft. Its first C-17 arrived in March 1996 and over the next year eight aircraft had been transferred from Charleston AFB. The number of C-17s assigned to the base as since risen to 15 aircraft

BELOW: Altus AFB is home to 13 C-17s, which are used by instructors of the 97th Air Mobility Wing to train the next generation of 'Moose' crews. USAF

as training expanded to cope with the growing fleet across the active duty and reserve components.

Boeing and other contractors have a strong presence at the airbase, assisting in the provision of training and providing flight simulators and other training devices.

Altus AFB has a long history as a training base, stretching back to 1943 when the then US Army Air Force opened the base as Altus Army Field. It closed after the war but re-opened in 1950 when the newly formed US Air Force was expanded to fight the Korean War. It subsequently became a Boeing B-52 Stratofortress base under Strategic Airlift Command

and then a silo field for Atlas nuclear armed ballistic missiles was installed.

In the 1960s, the airbase started its transition to its current training role when the then Military Airlift Command set up its schoolhouse for the Lockheed Martin C-5 Galaxy.

As well as C-17 training, the airbase is now home to Boeing KC-135 Stratotanker and Boeing KC-46 Pegasus training units. Many of its centralised services are run by the 97th AMW, with aircraft specific activities devolved to individual squadrons.

The 58th Airlift Squadron is focus of C-17 training and has its own

SUBORDINATE UNIT

58th Airlift Squadron

dedicated cadre of instructors to train both cockpit and cargo hold personnel. It shares many of the training resources with the 730th Air Mobility Training Squadron, which is an associate unit to provide training for C-17 personnel from the US Air Force Reserve and Air National Guard.

As well as training C-17, Altus AFB aircraft are regularly called upon to provide support for humanitarian and disaster relief missions in the Continental United States.

ABOVE: Trainee C-17 crews from Altus AFB flying all over the world during conversion course run from the Oklahoma base. USAF

BELOW: Loadmasters are trained at Altus AFB in the vital skills of securing cargo holds of C-17s. USAF

412TH TEST WING

Edwards AFB, California

Responsibility for the trials and testing of modifications and upgrades to the Boeing C-17A Globemaster III lies with the 418th Flight Test Squadron (FLTS). This unit is part of the US Air Force's Material Command's 412th Test Wing at Edwards AFB in California.

All modifications, new releases of software and capability upgrades have to be flight tested by the crews of the 418th FLTS to make sure they work as advertised and do not impact on the safety of the aircraft. The squadron's test pilots, and subject matter experts also work on other large transport and tanker aircraft in USAF service. The 418th FLTS usually borrows an aircraft from the active fleet when it needs to test new features on the C-17.

Increasingly, 418th FLTS has become involved in novel flight experiments to adapt the C-17 to new roles and missions. This regularly includes the dropping of space craft or large rockets to test their aerodynamics. Some of these, such as ballistic target missiles, are ignited after they are extracted from a C-17s rear cabin by a drogue parachute. The final parachute certification air drops of NASA's Orion space capsule also took place from a C-17 crewed by the 418th FLTS.

LEFT: 418th Flight Test Squadron pilots are routinely used to trial launches of rockets and space ships, including extended Medium Range Ballistic Missiles tests for the Missile Defence Agency, by deploying them out of a C-17s rear cargo ramp. USAF

Edwards AFB has had a long association with the C-17s and the first prototype, aircraft 87-0025, which was codenamed T-1, spent 20 years taking part in trials at the base after being delivered direct from the Long Beach assembly plant on September 15, 1991. After completing the C-17 flight test programme, the aircraft was repurposed into

a dedicated trials aircraft and supported many other flight and propulsion test programs for the USAF, NASA and others.

The 6517th Test Squadron was established in 1989 to perform flight testing on the new C-17. In 1992 it was redesignated the 417th Test Squadron and in October 1995 it became the 418th FLTS. At its peak, the C-17 flight test programme at Edwards AFB involved T-1 and five production standard aircraft.

SUBORDINATE UNIT

418th Flight Test Squadron

BELOW: C-17s are tested in a variety of extreme environments by the 418th Flight Test Squadron at training ranges around Edwards AFB. USAF

UNITED STATES AIR FORCE RESERVE

United States Air Force

315TH AIRLIFT WING (ASSOCIATE)

Joint Base Charleston, South Carolina

The US Air Force Reserve's 315th Airlift Wing is the associate unit of the active duty 437th Airlift Wing, sharing a fleet of 40 Boeing C-17A Globemaster III aircraft, maintenance and support infrastructure.

Under the associate wing concept, active duty and reserve personnel are routinely teamed together to fly join missions around the world, as well as running integrated training at the South Carolina base.

The wing traces its roots back to the 315th Troop Carrier Wing, Medium, which was formed in May 1952 as part of the US Far East Air Force in Japan. It was deactivated after the end the Korean War but stood up again in 1966 to serve in Vietnam. In 1973 it was re-activated as a reserve component unit to fly the Lockheed C-141 Starlifter.

During the 1990s, as the 437th Airlift Wing started to transition to the C-17, the reservists of the 315th Airlift Wing started to their own transition process to become the first reserve component unit to fly the new airlifter. Its last C-141 was retired in 2001 to complete the process.

Like its active-duty counter-part, the 315th Airlift Wing has three airlift squadrons, as well maintenance, operations, logistic, contingency response, aerial port, security, medical evacuation, communications and civil engineering units.

SUBORDINATE UNITS

300th Airlift Squadron

317th Airlift Squadron

701st Airlift Squadron

ABOVE: 315th Airlift Wing reserve crews joined a mass fly past of Joint Base Charleston C-17s over the Arthur Ravenel Bridge in 2008. USAF

LEFT: A yellow unit identification strip is applied to the tail of Joint Base Charleston C-17s. USAF

349TH AIR MOBILITY WING (ASSOCIATE)

Travis AFB, California

The US Air Force Reserve's 349th Air Mobility Wing is the associate unit of the active duty 60th Air Mobility Wing, sharing a fleet of 13 Boeing C-17A Globemaster III aircraft, maintenance and support infrastructure.

Under the associate wing concept, active duty and reserve personnel are routinely teamed together to fly join missions around the world, as well as running integrated training at the California airbase. It currently has a strength of 2,700 reserve airmen, who serve in a variety of roles alongside their active-duty counterpart on operations and training.

The wing traces its lineage back to the 349th Troop Carrier Group of World War Two, which operated in the European Theatre for the remainder of the war. It was reformed as a reserve airlift unit in 1949 and then transitioned to the fighter bomber role in 1953. Four years later it returned to the airlift role and during the Vietnam conflict was heavily involved in flying supply missions the Southeast Asian country using the Douglas C-124 Globemaster II.

In 1969, the wing re-located to Travis AFB in California and converted to the veteran Lockheed C-141 Starlifter and four years later began flying the Lockheed C-5 Galaxy. The first C-17 started to arrive at Travis AFB in summer of 2006 and both active duty and reserve crews started to convert to fly the new airlifter. In May 2006, the 301st Airlift Squadron converted from the C-5 to the C-17.

SUBORDINATE UNIT

301st Airlift Squadron

LEFT: A Travis AFB C-17 unloads a HIMARS rocket system during a US Army rapid mobility exercise.
USAF

BELOW: The US Air Force Reserve 349th Air Mobility Wing shares 13 C-17s with it active-duty counter parts in the 60th Air Mobility Wing.
USAF

445TH AIRLIFT WING

Wright-Patterson AFB, Ohio

LEFT: 445th Airlift Wing C-17s carry the insignia on their tails to commemorate that their home base is where Wilbur and Orville Wright conducted experimental test flights with the Wright Flyer III. USAF

The 445th Airlift Wing is a self-contained US Air Force Reserve unit, which solely operates the Boeing C-17A Globemaster III, and currently has nine of the giant airlifters assigned to it.

The present unit strength is approximately 1,700 officers, enlisted airmen and civilian personnel. Most of the wing personnel are traditional reservists, totalling 1,266 members, who serve in the military on a part-time basis, participating a minimum of one weekend a month as well as two-weeks of annual training each year. Augmenting the traditional reserve force is a team of approximately 230 airmen employed full-time as Air Reserve Technicians in the unit, nearly 90 Active Guard Reserve (AGR) members, and more than 90 civilians.

The wing traces its history back to 1952 when it was stood up as a fighter unit but transitioned to the airlift role later in the decade. It converted to the Lockheed C-141 Starlifter in 1973 but only moved to Wright-Patterson AFB in Ohio in October 1994. In 2005, the wing converted to fly the Lockheed C-5 Galaxy heavy airlifter.

It was announced in March 2010 that the 445th Airlift Wing would transition to the C-17. The first C-17 arrived in January 2011, and the wing flew its last Galaxy mission on September 28, 2011. The wing fully equipped with the C-17 in February 2012.

BELOW: Reserve C-17 crews from Wright Patterson AFB regularly practice air-to-air refuelling. USAF

446TH AIRLIFT WING (ASSOCIATE)

Joint Base Lewis-McChord, Washington

The US Air Force Reserve's 446th Airlift Wing is the associate unit of the active duty 437th Airlift Wing, sharing a fleet of 42 Boeing C-17A Globemaster III aircraft, maintenance and support infrastructure.

Under the associate wing concept, active duty and reserve personnel are routinely teamed together to fly joint missions around the world, as well as running integrated training at the Washington State airbase.

The wing's heritage includes being a World War Two bomber unit in the US Army Air Force. It reformed in 1948 as an airlift unit in the USAF reserve component.

In 1973, the 446th was reactivated and redesignated the 446th Military Airlift Wing (Associate), at McChord AFB in Washington State, flying the Lockheed C-141 Starlifter. It soon earned its nickname, the Rainier Wing. In February 1992, the wing was re-designated again, this time as the 446th Airlift Wing.

Currently the wing has fourteen squadrons, including three which fly the C-17 and work closely with their active-duty counterparts.

The wing began transitioning to the C17 in Globemaster III in July 1999 and the 728th Airlift Squadron was stood up as its flying unit to operate the C-17. It flew its first operational C-17 mission in November 1999 to Hanoi in Vietnam to recover the remains of fallen US airmen lost in the conflict in Southeast Asia.

SUBORDINATE UNITS

97th Airlift Squadron
313th Airlift Squadron
728th Airlift Squadron

LEFT: Reserve crews from the 446th Airlift Wing routinely take their aircraft to the Arctic and Antarctic regions in training and operational missions. USAF

452ND AIR MOBILITY WING

March ARB, California

The 452nd Airlift Wing was the first self-contained US Air Force Reserve unit to begin operating the Boeing C-17A Globemaster III in August 2005.

It has its own fleet 13 C-17 assigned to it to operate in support of Air Mobility Command's global mission.

During World War Two, its predecessor unit, the 452nd Bombardment Group (Heavy) was an Eighth Air Force Boeing B-17 Flying Fortress unit in England, stationed at RAF Deopham Green. Two of its officers, 1st Lieutenant Donald J. Gott and 2nd Lieutenant William E. Metzger, Jr were awarded the Medal of Honor for their heroic actions.

After World War Two it was reformed as a reserve bomber

SUBORDINATE UNIT

729th Airlift Squadron

unit, before transitioning to the airlift role in 1958. It moved to March AFB in 1976, flying McDonnell Douglas KC-10 Extender and Boeing KC-135 Stratotanker air-to-air refuelling tankers.

The wing's airlift unit, the 729th Airlift Squadron started to fly the C-141 in 1994 after relocating to March AFB from Norton AFB.

In August 2005, the wing received its first C-17 strategic airlifter, named "Spirit of California".

ABOVE: The 452nd Airlift Wing was the first self-contained US Air Force Reserve unit to receive the C-17 in 2005. USAF

LEFT: March AFB home to one of two reserve wings in California that operate the C-17. USAF

507TH AIR REFUELING WING

Tinker AFB, Oklahoma/ Altus AFB, Oklahoma

ABOVE: Lieutenant Colonel Erick Brough, 730th Air Mobility Training Squadron commander, practices low level flying in a C-17 in 2021 from Altus AFB. USAF

The 507th Air Refuelling Wing is the umbrella unit that oversees the training of US Air Force Reserve Boeing KC-135 Stratotanker tanker and Boeing C-17A Globemaster III crews from across the US Air Force Reserve and Air National Guard.

Training on the C-17 is conducted by a geographically separated unit, the 730th Air Mobility Training Squadron, which is based at Altus AFB in Oklahoma. It is a Formal Training Unit, where student C-17 pilots and loadmasters convert to fly the airlifter.

In June 2012, the 730th Air Mobility Training Squadron was activated at Altus AFB as an associate to the active duty 97th Air Mobility Wing. It was originally assigned to the 452nd Operations Group at March ARB. In August 2014, the unit was transferred under the command of the 507th Air Refueling Wing, located at Tinker AFB, but operational control of its training mission falls to the 97th Air Mobility Wing. The squadron's personnel are a mix of reservists and full-time reserve technicians who make up nearly 25% of the instructors at Altus. Roughly half the personnel instruct aircrew operating the Boeing C-17 Globemaster III and the other half focus on the Boeing KC-135 Stratotanker.

SUBORDINATE UNIT

730th Air Mobility Training Squadron (Altus AFB, Oklahoma)

RIGHT: Altus AFB in Oklahoma is home to all active duty and reserve component C-17 training. USAF

512TH AIRLIFT WING (ASSOCIATE)

Dover AFB, Delaware

The US Air Force Reserve's 512th Air Mobility Wing, known as the 'Liberty Wing', is the associate unit of the active duty 436th Air Mobility Wing, sharing a fleet of 13 Boeing C-17A Globemaster III aircraft, maintenance and support infrastructure.

Under the associate wing concept, active duty and reserve personnel are routinely teamed together to fly join missions around the world, as well as running integrated training at the Delaware airbase. Its reserve airmen, who serve in a variety of roles alongside their active-duty counterparts on operations and training.

The wing was first organised at Reading Municipal Airport in Pennsylvania in September 1949 as the 512th Troop Carrier Wing. A few months later, in April 1950, reserve operations at Reading ended when the wing transferred to New Castle County Airport, Delaware. In 1968, the wing moved to Dover AFB and became the associate unit, supporting the 436th Military Airlift Wing.

It first flew the Lockheed C-141 Starlifter up to 1973 and then the Lockheed C-5 Galaxy. In 2007, the wing began a new era in airlift when its 326th Airlift Squadron began flying the C-17 Globemaster III after it received their first C-17 on May 31, 2007. Since then, it has routinely operated around the world supporting US forces, including fly extensive missions to Iraq and Afghanistan.

SUBORDINATE UNIT

326th Airlift Squadron

ABOVE: Reserve C-17 crews from Dover AFB regularly spread their wings across the Atlantic and Pacific oceans during training and operational missions. USAF

LEFT: The 512th Air Mobility Wing is also known as the 'Liberty Wing'. USAF

514TH AIR MOBILITY WING (ASSOCIATE)

Joint Base McGuire-Dix-Lakehurst, New Jersey

LEFT: Reserve C-17 crews of the 514th Air Mobility Wing (Associate) often fly as members of mixed crews with their active-duty counterparts in the 305th Air Mobility Wing. USAF

The US Air Force Reserve's 514th Air Mobility Wing is the associate unit of the active duty 305th Air Mobility Wing, sharing a fleet of 13 Boeing C-17A Globemaster III aircraft, maintenance and support infrastructure.

Under the associate wing concept, active duty and reserve personnel are routinely teamed together to fly join missions around the world, as well as running integrated training at the Delaware airbase. Its 1,600 reserve airmen, serve in a variety of roles alongside their active-duty counterpart on operations and training.

The 514th Troop Carrier Wing was formed at Birmingham Municipal Airport in June 1949. It served in the Korean War flying Douglas C-46 Commando transport aircraft and then returned to its home base. In 1968, the wing was at McGuire AFB in New Jersey and received its first Lockheed C-141 Starlifter, just as the

unit was re-designated as a military airlift wing (associate). Five years later it received its first Lockheed C-5 Galaxy and subsequently was equipped with McDonnell Douglas KC-10 Extender tanker aircraft.

When McGuire AFB's active-duty units began to transition from the C-141 to the C-17 in 2004, the 732nd Airlift Squadron's crews also started to convert

to the new aircraft. It was heavily involved in supporting America's wars in Iraq and Afghanistan and in 2008 became the first reserve C-17 squadron to send aircrews on temporary duty (TDY) support the C-17 Rotational Airlift Mission at Ramstein Airbase in Germany. From there the reserve crews flew mission across Europe and Middle East.

BELOW: Reserve Citizen Airmen with the 514th Air Mobility Wing stand in formation at Joint Base McGuire-Dix-Lakehurst during the training assembly. USAF

SUBORDINATE UNIT

732nd Airlift Squadron

911TH AIRLIFT WING

Pittsburgh ARS, Pennsylvania

ABOVE: Pittsburgh has a long tradition of citizen aviators serving in the US Air Force Reserve, which continues with the 911th Airlift Wing. USAF

The 911th Airlift Wing is a self-contained US Air Force Reserve unit, which solely operates the Boeing C-17A Globemaster III, and currently has eight of the giant airlifters assigned to it.

The present unit strength is approximately 1,220 officers, enlisted airmen and civilian personnel. The base also employs approximately 350 Department of Defense civilians. Many of these civilians hold a dual status as reserve technicians and nearly 100 contractors provide airbase support.

The squadron was first formed during World War Two as the 758th Bombardment Squadron of the US Army Air Force. It served in the Mediterranean Theatre of Operations, where it participated in the strategic bombing campaign against Germany and earned a Distinguished Unit Citation for its actions.

By 1957, the unit was part of the reserve component, as the 758th Troop Carrier Squadron, and was based at Greater Pittsburgh Airport in Pennsylvania.

The unit converted to Lockheed C-130A Hercules airlifter in 1980 and then the C-130H aircraft in 1987. It was renamed 911th Airlift Group in 1992 and then the 911th Airlift Wing in 1994.

In April 2019, the 911th Airlift Wing received its first three C-17s to begin its conversion to its new aircraft. It was the last USAF unit to convert to fly the iconic airlifter.

SUBORDINATE UNIT

758th Airlift Squadron

In 2023 one of the 911st Airlift Wing's C-17s had D-Day 'invasion stripes' applied in honour of veterans of the invasion of France in World War Two. USAF

AIR NATIONAL GUARD

Air National Guard

105TH AIRLIFT WING

Stewart ANGB, New York

The 105th Airlift Wing is a unit of the New York Air National Guard, which has been based at Stewart Air National Guard Base at Newburgh, New York, since 1983 as a self-contained unit.

Its history dates back to its founding as the 504th Fighter Squadron which was located at Westchester County Airport in May 1946.

In 1961, the unit took on the cargo transport mission for a decade before converting to fly forward air control missions during the Vietnam war. In 1984 the 105th Airlift Wing returned to airlift missions flying the Lockheed C-5A Galaxy. The last of the wing's C-5As departed its Hudson Valley home for the final time in September 2012.

Its first Boeing C-17A Globemaster III arrived at Stewart ANGB, on July 18, 2011, in time for a roll-out ceremony the following month when two C-17s were put on public display.

The 105th played an important role in New York State's COVID-19

LEFT: Stewart Air National Guard Base is home to the 105th Airlift Wing. USAF

SUBORDINATE UNIT

137th Airlift Squadron

pandemic response in 2010, flying dozens of American citizens, from all over the world, back using Negative Pressure Containers.

The 137th Airlift Squadron participated in Operation Allies Refuge, the evacuation from Kabul, Afghanistan in August 2021. On their final Afghanistan mission, aircrew members of the squadron airlifted 13 fallen US servicemen from Kabul.

BELOW: The New York Air National Guard's C-17 crews have participated in operations around the world with their active-duty counterparts since they converted to the airlifter in 2017. USAF

145TH AIRLIFT WING

Charlotte ANGB, North Carolina

The North Carolina Air National Guard's 154th Airlift Wing is a self-contained unit, which has state and federal missions. As well as being an airlift squadron equipped with the Boeing C-17A Globemaster III, the wing contains specialist aeromedical, operations, maintenance, medical and security units.

Its 156th Airlift Squadron provides tactical airlift for airborne forces, as well as moving personnel, equipment, and supplies. The squadron also provides evacuation of refugees and aeromedical patients within a theatre of operations.

This squadron traces its origins back to December 1942, when the 360th Fighter Squadron was formed as part of the US Army Air Forces. At the end of World War II, it was redesignated the 156th Fighter Squadron and assigned to the National Guard, flying the Republic P-47 Thunderbolt.

From 1961 through to 2017 it took on the airlift mission and for more than 45 years flew versions of the Lockheed C-130 Hercules tactical airlifter.

The wing's last C-130H departed on December 22, 2017 before the wing received its first of eight C-17 Globemaster III on April 7, 2018. Since then, the unit's aircraft have routinely taken part in USAF Air Mobility Command tasking around the world.

ABOVE: The 145th Airlift Wing conducted a medical evacuation exercise with the Columbian air force in 2023. USAF

SUBORDINATE UNIT
156th Airlift Squadron

The North Carolina Air National Guard's 145th Airlift Wing has flown the C-17 since 2018 and regularly trains with US Army airborne units based in the Southwest of the United States. USAF

154TH WING

Joint Base Pearl Harbor–Hickam, Hawaii

The 154th Wing is headquartered at Joint Base Pearl Harbor-Hickam on Oahu in the Pacific state of Hawaii. It comprises of nearly 1,900 full- and part-time airmen and is the largest Hawaii Air National Guard (HIANG) organisation, consisting of a headquarters element and 12 squadrons.

The 204th Airlift Squadron is 154th Wing dedicated airlift unit of the HIANG, which operates as an associate unit with the active duty 535th Airlift Squadron, also based at Joint Base Pearl Harbor-Hickam, providing 40 percent of the Team Hickam's C-17 flight crews.

It was established in 1994 to provide the HIANG with a theater airlift capability and to support joint exercises in Hawaii with US Army and US Marine Corps units.

The squadron supports operational training, provides paratroop and tactical air drop capability, and delivers relief supplies following natural disasters.

Originally, the squadron was equipped with Lockheed C-130 Hercules tactical airlifters, which were formally retired in a farewell ceremony at Hickam Air Force Base in February 2006. It then transitioned to the C-17, making it the first joint USAF and Air National Guard C-7 unit outside of the Continental USA.

As well as flying conventional airlift missions of US Air Mobility Command, the squadron has worked closely with the Department of Defense Human Space Flight Support (HSFS) Office to develop and implement long-range, high-speed tactics for contingency location, identification, rescue and recovery of US and partner-nation astronauts under the direction of US Space Command.

SUBORDINATE UNIT

204th Airlift Squadron (Associate)

RIGHT: Moving US Marines around the Pacific region is an important mission for the 154th Wing's C-17s. USAF

BELOW: A C-17 flown by 154th Wing reservists overflies Pearl Harbor naval base on the Hawaiian Island of Oahu. USAF

164TH AIRLIFT WING

Memphis ANGB, Tennessee

RIGHT: Moving US Army troops rapidly to crisis zones is regularly practiced by 164th Airlift Wing crews. USAF

SUBORDINATE UNIT

155th Airlift Squadron

164th Airlift Wing traces its history back to 1946 when the Secretary of War authorised the Adjutant of General of Tennessee to organise an air unit of the National Guard in Memphis and in December 1946 the 155th Fighter Squadron was formally activated.

On April 1, 1961, the wing converted the military airlift role, flying the Boeing C-97 Stratofreighter and then transitioned to the Douglas C-124 Globemaster II. In 1974 it converted to fly the Lockheed C-130A Hercules tactical airlifter.

The C-130s were transferred to other units in April 1992 when the unit received the first of eight Lockheed C-141 Starlifter aircraft and twelve years later the squadron began operating the Lockheed C-5A Galaxy.

The first of eight Boeing C-17A Globemaster IIIs arrived at Memphis in November 2012.

BELOW: The Tennessee Air National Guard has operated the C-17s since 2015. USAF

The 164th Airlift Wing is located at the Memphis Air National Guard Base at Memphis International Airport in the southern state of Tennessee. This airport is known as the 'America's Aerotropolis' because of the extensive aerospace industry network based in the state. Many of the guardsmen who serve in the 164th Airlift Wing have civilian employment in the local aerospace industry.

167TH AIRLIFT WING

Shepherd Field ANGB, West Virginia

The 167th Airlift Wing is a unit of the West Virginia Air National Guard, stationed at Shepherd Field Air National Guard Base in Martinsburg, which is equipped with eight Boeing C-17A Globemaster III airlifters.

The wing traces its history back 1943 when the 359th Fighter Group was formed to fly long range fighter sweeps to protect US Army Air Force bombers flying missions over Germany.

At the end of World War Two, the West Virginia Air National Guard took on the group's traditions. Its 167th Fighter Squadron initially flew the North American P-51 Mustang and then the jet powered North American F-86 Sabre fighters. The unit's motto, 'Mountaineer Pride Worldwide', sums up its global role but strong link to rural West Virginia.

It took on the airlift mission in 1961 and from 1971 to 2006 flew versions of the Lockheed C-130

SUBORDINATE UNIT

167th Airlift Squadron

Hercules tactical transport. In March 2002, West Virginia Senator Robert Byrd announced that the unit would transition to the Lockheed C-5 Galaxy strategic aircraft. On December 4, 2006, the first C-5 aircraft assigned to the unit landed at Shepherd Field.

The wing has since retired its fleet of C-5 aircraft and in 2015 started to receive its first C-17 transport aircraft.

The West Virginia Air National Guard 167th Airlift Wing has had an airlift role since 1961, flying a C-5 and C-130 aircraft before it converted to C-17 in 2015. USAF

BELOW: 'Mountaineer Pride Worldwide' is the motto of the 167th Airlift Wing. USAF

172ND AIRLIFT WING

Allen C. Thompson Field ANGB, Mississippi

The Mississippi Air National Guard was formed in September 1939, with the 153rd Observation Squadron as its first unit.

The 172nd Airlift Wing traces its history back to 1953 when the 183rd Tactical Reconnaissance Squadron was first established in Mississippi. In 1957, the unit has transitioned from its original night photo mission to become the 183rd Aeromedical Transport Squadron, which became part of the 172nd Air Transport Group in 1963. It then flew several iconic transport aircraft, including Lockheed C-121 Constellation, Douglas C-124 Globemaster II, Lockheed C-130 Hercules and Lockheed C-141 Starlifter. It then became the 172nd Airlift Wing in 1995.

In February 2003, the wing's 183rd Airlift Squadron retired its last Starlifter in preparation for the arrival of the wing's first Boeing C-17 Globemaster III. On December 17, 2003, Lieutenant General Daniel James III, Director, Air National Guard, handed off the 'keys' of the first C-17, aircraft 02-1112, to Major General James H. Lipscomb III, adjutant general of the Mississippi National Guard. This was the first Globemaster III assigned to the Air National Guard and was named the 'Spirit of the Minutemen', in honour of the original colonial era American militiamen.

The 183rd Airlift Squadron is currently based at Allen C. Thompson Field Air National Guard Base in Mississippi and operates 12 C-17 aircraft.

ABOVE: 'May the Airlift Force be with you'. Families' day at the Allen C. Thompson Field Air National Guard Base in Mississippi. USAF

SUBORDINATE UNIT

183rd Airlift Squadron

The 172nd Airlift Wing was the first Air National Guard to operate the C-17, after receiving its first aircraft in 2003. USAF

176TH WING

Joint Base Elmendorf-Richardson, Alaska

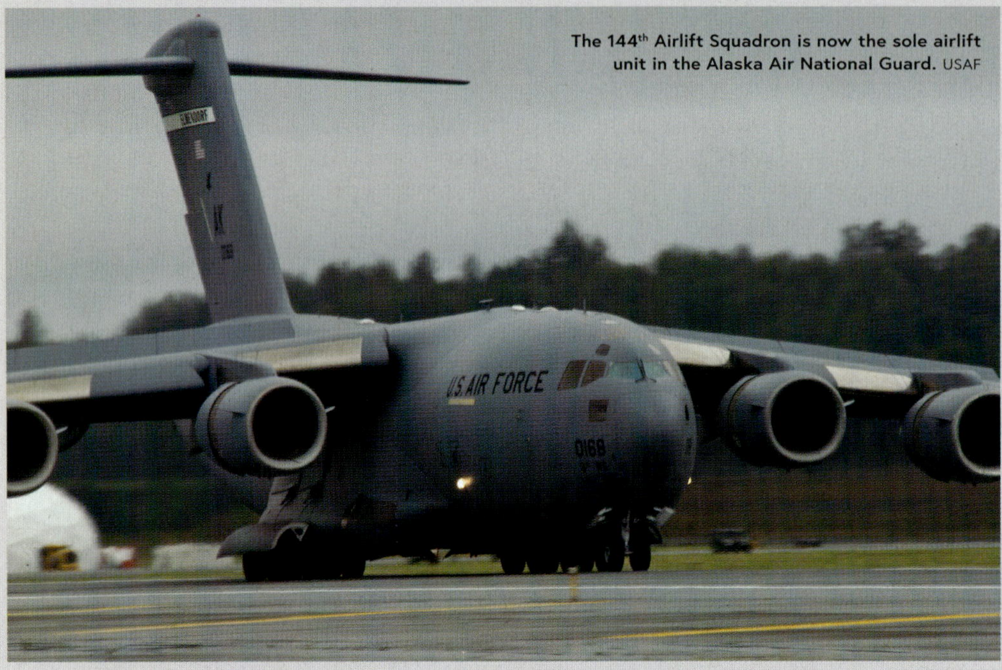

The 144th Airlift Squadron is now the sole airlift unit in the Alaska Air National Guard. USAF

SUBORDINATE UNIT
144th Airlift Squadron

The USAF presence in the northern state of Alaska is concentrated at Joint Base Elmendorf-Richardson (JBER), close to the 49th State's capital, Anchorage. The Alaska's Air National Guard's 176th Wing has an airlift, rescue and air defence role, with a strength of 1,500 personnel.

Its 144th Airlift Squadron was one of the first Air National Guard units to be organised as an associate unit, sharing aircraft, maintenance and support infrastructure with the active duty 517th Airlift Squadron.

176th Wing began C-17 operations in the summer of 2007, with its 249th Airlift Squadron formally declaring initial operational capability (IOC) on September 17, 2009, followed by full operational capability (FOC) in first months of 2012.

In a shake-up of the Alaska Air National Guard's airlift units in 2017, the Lockheed Martin C-130H Hercules operated by 144th Airlift Squadron, were slated to be retired from service. As the 144th Squadron was the more senior unit, it was decided to transfer its unit title and traditions to the 249th Squadron so the Alaska-based C-17 unit was renamed on August 4, 2018.

The 144th Airlift Squadron's current authorised strength is 70 total personnel with 34 officers and 36 enlisted members, mostly comprising C-17 aircrew members.

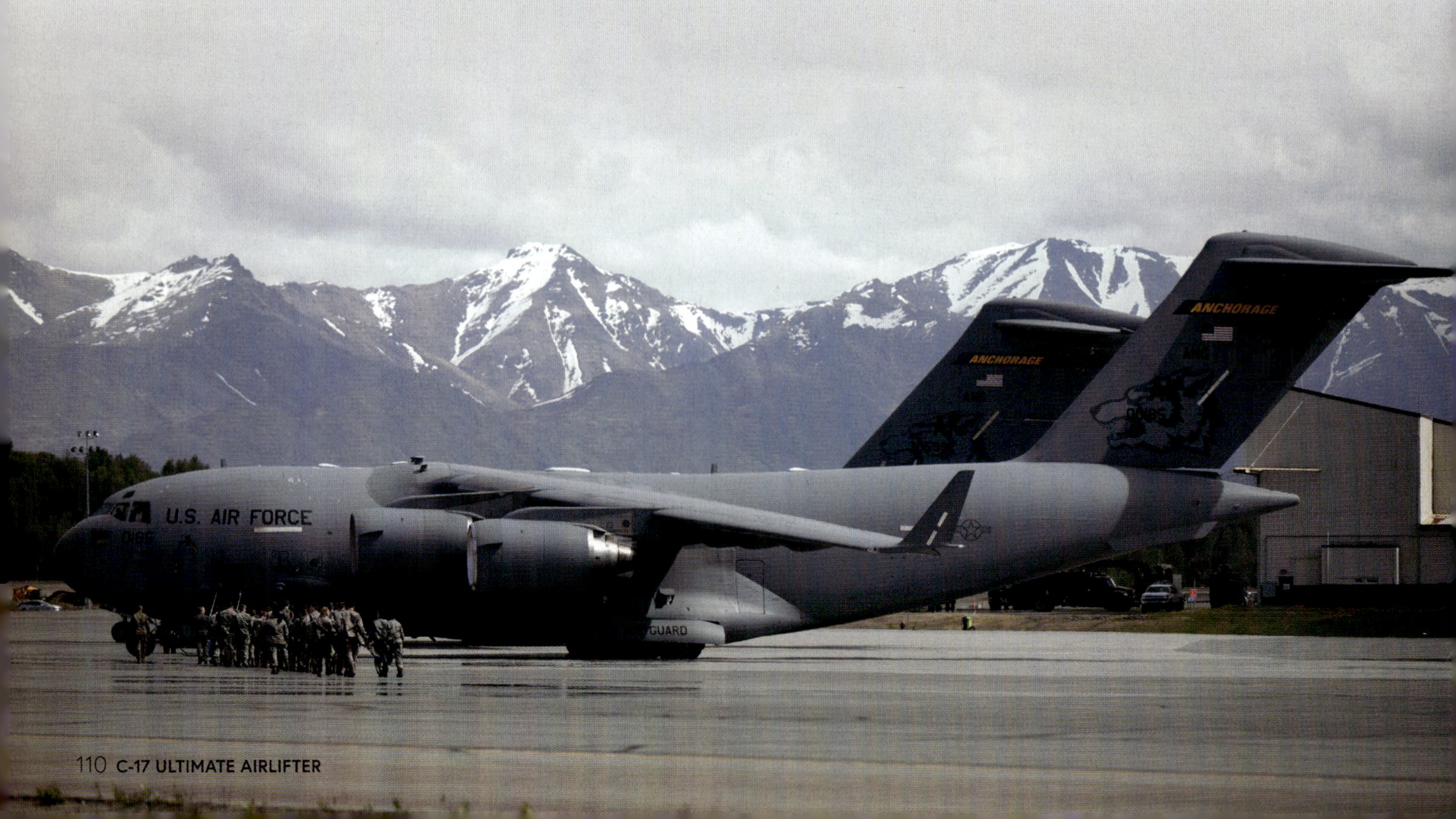

BELOW: The 144th Airlift Squadron is an associate unit of the active duty 517th Airlift Wing, sharing a fleet of eight C-17s. USAF

C-17 FOREVER?

The Future of the Globemaster

As the Boeing C-17A Globemaster III approaches the 35th anniversary of its first flight, some attention has focused on what could possibly replace the 'ultimate airlifter'. Given that the USAF expects to keep some of its C-17s flying into the 2050s, thinking about a next generation airlifter is not an immediate priority for the Pentagon.

The programme to field next generation US Air Force airlift capabilities is still at an early stage and it's unclear if it will be pursued under the tentative Next-Generation Airlift (NGAL) title, or if it will be reconfigured under the name Next-Generation Airlift System (NGALS), to better represent the fact that it will involve a family of different platforms and capabilities.

At the heart of the pace of these projects will be whether the current C-17 fleet will continue to put up with its operational tempo. Operation Allies Refuge in 2021 stressed the C-17 fleet considerably, adding considerable flying hours and significant airframe fatigue to around half of the USAF's airframe. A major effort to transfer airlift activity to other USAF Air Mobility Command aircraft and commercial airlines was launched after the Kabul airlift to restore form stability to the C-17 fleet. It is not clear yet if the current regime of maintenance attention will mitigate this heavy usage and bring the fleet back to a long-term sustainable basis.

The USAF currently gets tremendous value out of its C-17s and only once maintenance costs start to spike will it begin considering whether to buy something new. First of all, it will look to a mid-life upgrade (MLU), which is likely to include re-sparing wings, new engines, a new avionics system and more modern defensive systems. As an aircraft that was designed in the 1980s and manufactured between 1991 and 2015, obsolescence of basic components is a major issue in the cost of sustaining the aircraft. A constant drive to find modern »

Size Matters: When looking to replace the C-17, customers have to consider the type of cargoes they need to carry. MoD/Crown Copyright equivalent components, for things such as wiring looms, electrical systems and mechanical systems, will play an important part in driving out costs from any effort to keep the C-17 in service. The next issue will be whether this should be a fleet-wide effort or just on high hours' airframes. Re-engining the aircraft to improve fuel efficiency and reduce support costs will be an important development in any drive to keep the C-17 in service.

Only when all those routes have been explored, will attention turn to a new airframe. A big chunk of the C-17s mission profile could be carried out by converted civilian airlines but the C-17 does things that no civilian aircraft can do. It carries heavy and bulky cargo into austere airstrips and unloads it without any external assistance. This is a unique military requirement, and the USAF paid a premium to get these capabilities, in the shape of the C-17. Time and again the C-17 has done things that no aircraft could do.

C-17 pilots routinely comment that "size is a quality all of its own" and this points to another big aircraft that can lift 50 tonnes or more, combined with the need for a robust undercarriage to land on dirt strips and the ability to turn on a penny on the ground, without tow trucks – all of which point to a bespoke military airframe.

The current obsession with drone technology has led some observers to talk about future airlifters being unmanned platforms, but airlift is an essentially human business, needing crews to make rapid judgements on the state of airfields, the condition of passengers and threat assessments. A manned airlifter seems likely.

The USAF already operates the Northrop Grumman B-2 Spirit and is buying the B-21 Raider, which are both essentially 'flying wings'. There have been suggestions that this type of technology could be applied to the airlift mission to create a 'blended wing' airlifter. Given the increased threats from enemy air defences, incorporating so-called stealth, or low observable, technology would appear to have some benefits.

Despite a great deal of conceptual and early design work, there appear to be many hurdles to building a next-generation airlifter in a cost-effective manner.

This all points to the replacement for the C-17 being a new C-17. Boeing has reportedly been approached by a number of customers, believed to be Saudi Arabia and Japan, »

BOTTOM: Digital modelling and computer-aided design technology will be central to building the next generation of airlifter. USAF

BELOW: Two prototypes of the Advanced Medium STOL Transport aircraft were built in a project to find a replacement for the C-130 in the 1970s. Mike Freer

ABOVE: Boeing's X-48B blended wing demonstrator made its first flight in July 2007. NASA

LEFT: The replacement for the C-17 might well be another C-17. USAF

ABOVE: Boeing's colourful X-48B Blended Wing Body technology demonstrator shows off its unique triangular lines while parked on Rogers Dry Lake adjacent to NASA Dryden. *NASA*

to consider re-opening production of the C-17. Although the old Douglas Aircraft Company's plant in Long Beach, where all 275 C-17s were assembled, has been sold off, Boeing has plenty of capacity in its civilian airliner assembly facilities to restart C-17 production. It has kept it designs and engineering tools so could in theory get back into the C-17 assembly business.

'Going back to the future' might work for a handful aircraft built to an old design for a few niche customers with a dozen or so aircraft but if Boeing wants to set up a long-term business that has the prospect of replacing the 100 or so C-17s built for the USAF in 1990s then it needs to incorporate next-generation technology from the start.

The C-17 needs to be re-engineered from the start to incorporate modern aero-structures and assembly techniques. Then a fully digital aircraft needs to fielded, along with a 21st century powerplant. These things would drive out weight from the design – reducing cost, as well as improving performance and efficiency.

This transformed C-17 would still do its unique mission but at a fraction of the cost of keeping ageing airframes in service. Only an order from the USAF would provide the scale of investment needed to pay for such a project.

The C-17 has proved such a rugged and effective aircraft that the world aerospace industry will struggle to come up with a true replacement. It has proved to be the ultimate airlifter.

In August 2023, the USAF selected innovative aerospace startup JetZero and Northrop Grumman to design, build and fly a full-scale blended wing body aircraft (BWB), which aims to demonstrate enhanced capabilities for improved efficiency, endurance and cargo capacity on multi-mission military and commercial platforms. *Northrop Grumman*